NOTED SPIRITUALISTS

OF 1895

Reverend Karen L. Heasley
with
Susan Urbanek Linville

This book was inspired by *Our Noted Workers*, a collection of photographs compiled by Jennie Hagan Jackson, printed by The Dean Printing and Publishing Company and Grand Rapids Engraving Company, 1 January 1895. We have reproduced the original photographs and are republishing them with our accompanying biographies of the Spiritualists portrayed.

In the original album Jennie wrote, "The album is dedicated to my mother, Janett Hagan, and the many dear friends who will enjoy looking at the faces of these variously gifted and well known workers in our glorious cause. We have often wished, as you have, for a large album in which all our representative people in spiritualistic work might appear, and from that wish has come to this, our first effort, in part covering this ground. If it is received with the same kindness by which it has so far been supported, we can ask no more. Especially are we indebted to Mr. Wm. F. Nye, Hon. A. Gaston, J. R. Francis, John Day, Mrs. M. E. Wallace, Geo. W Taylor, and all whose pictures are within, for kindness rendered us."

This book is dedicated to Jennie Hagan Jackson and all the Spiritualists who have gone before us and those who diligently work today to bring the physical and spiritual worlds together.

Contents

JAMES MADISON & MARGARET THERESA ALLEN

James Madison Allen was born to Galen and Maria Allen in East Bridgewater, Massachusetts in 1837. He was educated in the common schools, graduated and became a teacher. James participated in the Civil War for about one and half years before deserting. He married Cordelia Fanny Sampson in 1862 while living in East Bridgewater.they had one child, Loverneet, who was born in 1863 and died in 1879 of Typhoid fever. It's unclear what happened to the marriage. He and Fanny "Allyn," who became a notable medium, lived apart not long after their marriage.

In 1868, James married Sarah Spaulding. He became a lecturer on Spiritualism about that time and wrote while in trance. James was listed as a Spiritualist Lecturer in the *Banner of Light* for over two decades. During the 1870s, He lived in Massachusetts during the 1870s and New Jersey in the 1880s. He was Secretary of the First Spiritualist Society in Ancora, New Jersey for a time.

James married his third wife, Margaret Theresa, around 1800 and they made their home in Springfield, Missouri. The Allens were delegates to the First National Delegate Convention of Spiritualists held in Chicago in 1893.

James published a 92-page book of essays from his automatic writings from 1861 to 1864 entitled, *Essays; Philosophical, and Practical from the Higher Life*. They were an "argument on behalf of a continuous life after the close of our earthly career." Other publications noted in the *Pittsburg Kansan*, 26 March 1896, were *Messages from the Spiritual Congress through the Mediumship of James Madison Allen, Organic Basis of the Spiritual Co-operative Brotherhood*, and *Principal Reasons for Entertaining the Vegetarian or Fruitarian Principle*.

2

The Indianapolis Journal, 3 April 1896, wrote "Professor James Madison Allen, of this city, gave a short talk this morning on spiritualism. He was followed by Mrs. M. T. Allen, his wife. They are the only two mediums in attendance at the conference. Prof. Allen is one of the leading spiritualists of the State, and has just issued a pamphlet of six essays, purporting to come through him from those in the spirit land. He is a patriarch in appearance and is a power in the association."

James died in 1909 in Springfield, Missouri at age of 72. His obituary in the *Springfield News-Leader*, 25 August 1909, stated, "He was engaged nearly all of his life as a lecturer. He was prominent in the Spiritualist movement and in late years had devoted all of his time to that line of work. Mr. Allen possessed decided opinion on religious matters and spiritual affairs, being a close student and a writer and lecturer of considerable note."

C. FANNIE ALLYN

Cordelia Fannie Sampson was born in 1841 to Obadiah and Martha Sampson in Derby, Connecticut. She married James Madison Allen, a teacher, in 1862 while living in E. Bridgewater, Massachusetts. They had one child, Loverneet, who was born in 1863 and died in 1879 of Typhoid fever. James Allen was in the Civil War for about one and half years before deserting. It's unclear what happened to their marriage. Fannie refers to herself as married in the 1870 and 1880 censuses while she is living at her parents' home. She also spelled her name Allyn.

In the 1870 census, Fannie listed her employment as a Trance Medium. During the 1870s through the 1890s, while she lived in Massachusetts, she was a guest at most of the major Spiritualists camps in New England, including Onset Bay, Lake Pleasant, Highland Lake Grove, Silver Lake Grove, and Lake Sunapee. She also spoke at Spiritualist meetings in Boston and Fall River. She was author at least four hymns, including "Hail we the thought that moves the age," and "Ring the bells of mercy."

The *Democratic Press*, 27 December 1877, Ravenna, Ohio reported that, "Mrs. C. Fannie Allyn, of Stoneham, Mass., will give an improvised Lecture and Poem, upon any rational theme, presented by the audience on Thursday evening at Citizen's Hall, Mantua Station. All are invited."

The Boston Globe, 4 April 1904, published some of her lecture at a Spiritualist meeting. "'Easter Sunday is older than Christianity, Mrs. C. Fannie Allyn told the children of the Boston Spiritualists' lyceum at the anniversary exercises in Friendship Hall, Tremont and Berkeley streets, yesterday afternoon."

"'I am glad to recognize that we are pagan as well as partly Christian,' she continued. 'I recognize Easter astrologically long before Jesus came on earth. I recognize it with the Druids and with the minerals and with all the natural world. I don't celebrate the resurrection of one whom some of you worship as your Lord and Savior, but I celebrate the birth of aspiration and liberty.'"

The *Washington Herald,* 4 December 1915, listed her appearance at the First Spiritualist Church in the Pythian Temple where she was still lecturing and giving spiritual readings at the age of 71. Fannie passed on to the spirit world in 1927. She died in bed after being overcome with smoke from an overheated stove. Along with Spiritualism, she was also active in the G.A.R. Women's Relief Corps, being president of the Stoneham branch.

WILLIAM H. AND EVELINA P. BACH

William H. Bach, born in 1864 in Wisconsin to Edward and Frances Bach. He married Evalina (Evie) P. Foote from Parishville, New York in 1887. They lived in St Paul, Missouri in the late 1880s and early 1890s and had no children. William was active in Mesmeric and Spiritualist circles in the 1890s. He spoke at places like the St. Paul Spiritual Alliance, the First Phenomenal Society of Springfield, Missouri, and to Spiritualists in Atchison, Kansas.

The National Spiritualist Association of Churches was founded as the National Spiritualist Association of the United States of America (NSA) in 1893 during a convention in Chicago, Illinois. William was one of the NSA's first leaders along with Harrison D. Barrett, Luther V. Moulton, Cora L. V. Scott, and James Martin Peebles.

William and Evalina moved to the Lily Dale, New York area in the late 1890s. They attended the 1897 Spiritualists convention in Washington, D.C. where William was elected treasurer for the lyceum. The following year, William and Evie became the first editors of *The Sunflower,* published from 1898—1909, It was a semimonthly, then weekly, then semimonthly again newsletter published by A. Gaston and F. G. Neelin, by the Sunflower Publishing Co., and then by Hamburg Publishing Co. It was individually owned by William but functioned as the journal for the Cassadaga Camp meeting and Lily Dale. The Sunflower Pagoda was also built in 1898 by William. It is located midway between the Grand Hotel and the Auditorium and carried a complete stock of books, stationery, and other camping necessities.

William authored several publications, including: *A History of Cassadaga Camp,* printed as a premium for *The Sunflower* in 1899,

Mediumship and its Development, How to Mesmerize to Assist Development and *Big Bible Stories.*

In his book on mediumship, he wrote: "All manifestations of natural law are the result of Natural Conditions. We do not think there is a single reader of this book who will deny this premise. Our premise must be correct or our reasoning will be wrong. We are all, more or less, hero worshippers and it is hard to reach a solid, practical belief, throw all superstition to the winds and look at the practical side of things, which, to some, seem sacred."

In 1905, William and Evie were listed as printers in the New York Census. The Buffalo Times, 30 June 1907, reported," We regret that Mr. W.H. Bach, editor of 'The Sunflower,' advertises his plant and paper for sale, on account of ill health. It will be difficult to get another Mr. Bach. He is peculiarly gifted to do just that work."

It's unclear what happened to William. It's possible that he married another woman and moved to California. In 1910, Evie was still using the last name Bach, was listed as a widow living with her mother in New York state, and was employed as a businesswoman. In 1925, she was still running a souvenir shop in Lily Dale.

JOSEPH OSGOOD BARRETT

Joseph O. Barret was born in Canaan, Maine in 1823 to Joseph and Olive Barrett, one of their seven children. He was educated in botany and forestry, but after experiencing visions he became interested in mesmerism and trances. He trained for the ministry in the Universalist Church, and at the same time continued to practice mediumship.

Joseph married Olive S. Moore in 1853. The couple had four children while they moved from one location to the next, including Detroit, Michigan and Franklin Grove, Illinois. When Joseph admitted to a congregation in Illinois about his interest in Spiritualism, it caused an uproar in the church. He eventually lost his position with the church. The family moved again, settling in Wisconsin where he was a lecturer, writer, forestry expert, and editor of the Chicago newspaper, *The Spiritual Republic*. He wrote mainly about religion, but also about women's rights and botany.

Joseph was listed in the *Banner of Light* as an active lecturer in the Spiritualist community in the late 1860s and 1870s. He was a contributor to the *Spiritual Rostrum*, a delegate to the American Association of Spiritualists at their 1873 Chicago meeting, and was a speaker at the Michigan State Spiritualists Association in 1866.

Unfit to fight in the Civil War, he published the *Eau Claire Free Press* during that time. His other publications included, *Spiritual Pilgrim: a Biography of J. M. Peebles*, *Looking Beyond: A Souvenir of Love to the Bereft of Every Home*, and *Social Freedom: Marriage as It Is, and as It Should Be*. He also wrote a book about "Old Abe" the war eagle of the 8th Wisconsin Regiment. He edited Spiritualist hymnals and was involved with the American Spiritualist Publishing Co. as one of their editors.

In his book, *Looking Beyond: A Souvenir of Love to the Bereft of Every Home*, he wrote, "Herein you will find a 'Sunny philosophy,' 'a balm for every wounded heart.' Its sweet truths, and its consoling revelations from the 'better land,' will be needed by all. For we are all journeying thither and do ask for light to shine upon the way. Mine is humble,--but a single ray,-- while the great sun of heavenly benediction remains unmeasured. I may show you, perhaps, where its founts of divine baptism are. 'Come and see.'"

In 1881, he moved to Browns Valley, Minnesota and focused on his interest in forestry. In 1890, he was elected secretary of the State Forestry Association. His Annual Tree Planters' Manual encouraged tree culture throughout the prairie sections of the state. He was also sent by the Minnesota World's Fair commission to personally supervise the state's Forestry exhibit at the World's Fair in Chicago in 1892.

After an active life in both forestry and Spiritualism, Joseph passed away peacefully February 8, 1898, in Browns Valley, Minnesota.

Jacob C. Batdorf

Jacob C. Batdorf was born in 1833 in Champaign County Ohio to Jacob and Christina Batdorf on 21 June 1895. He married Susan Brown in 1852 and Zelia Helen Fowler in 1889. During the Civil War, he was an assistant surgeon in the 11th Iowa Infantry in 1862-1863.

Jacob ran the Magnetic Institute in Grand Rapids, Michigan. He advertised in many newspapers around the country and spiritualist publications. Later, two of his sons joined him.

In 1895, he was arrested for mail fraud. According to the *Detroit Free Press*, "J. C. Batdorf, a spiritualist physician and proprietor of a medicine factory, was arrested here last night on complaint of the United States Post Office Inspector Larmour, charged with using the mails fraudulently. Batdorf had been advertising in various spiritualist papers that if disease-inflected people would write a letter inclosing a lock of their hair he would diagnose their case and put them in way of relief."

"Batdorf admits all facts but says his practice is scientific, and he merely made mistakes sometimes, which all mortals, however scientific are liable to do."

The case never came to trial and, in 1901, Larmour charged Jacob again. This time he was fined $300 and sentenced to 6 months jail time. He moved to Berkeley California in 1905. Ads for the Magnetic Institute were still running in the papers. He died in January of 1928 at the age of 94.

J. FRANK BAXTER

Josiah Francis Baxter was born to Josiah and Elizabeth Baxter in 1841 in Plymouth, Massachusetts. He married Eliza C. Holmes about 1862 and worked as a schoolteacher in Plymouth, Winchester, Nantucket and Amesbury. They had one daughter, Elizabeth, who married Otto Baron.

Frank's interest in Spiritualism began sometime around 1870. In 1875, he taught a course of six lectures. Soon after, he began to deliver addresses at New England Spiritualist camps, including, "The Reality of Spiritualism," given in 1876 at Shawsheen Grove.

By 1877, Frank was listed as a test medium at the Onset Bay Grove Spiritualist camp. *The Boston Globe,* 23 July 1877, reported that, "Among them was a communication purporting to come from a girl named Matilda Frances Lyons. Through Mr. Baxter she recalled several things of her life on earth. Her father and mother, who were both present, responded to a question of the speaker, and asserted that what had been said was true, every word."

Frank was known as one "who has won golden opinions for his eloquence of speech and song, and for his mediumistic gifts, and lectures at the Brooklyn Institute." His work as a lecturer and medium continued through the 1880s and 1890s. He frequently attended Lake Pleasant and Cassadaga Lake/Lily Dale. One address at Onset Bay was entitled: "The Rise and Progress of Modern Spiritualism and its Demands upon its Advocate."

A booklet of one of his lectures was printed in 1893 entitled: "The Development of Spiritualism and its Demands upon its Recipients." In it he wrote, "Spiritualism should be presented by competent lecturers, exemplified by honest mediums, demonstrated by positive manifestations, not only in every city, but in every town throughout the

United States, and our efforts should ever be bent in such direction. Our best literature should also be extended through some system to all these places. Our lecturers and workers should always find a welcome in every place, sought, encouraged, and pleasantly environed, instead of finding themselves left apart and treated as strangers."

Frank was present at the Ohio State Spiritualist convention in May of 1897. He participated with other well-known Spiritualists: Rev. Moses Hull, of Massachusetts, Maggie Waite of California, Hon. L. V. Moulton of Grand Rapids, Mich., and Mrs. Cora L. V. Richmond of Chicago.

Frank's wife, Eliza, died in 1897, but Frank continued with his lectures. He traveled from Maine to the Midwest, including: Indiana, Ohio, and Missouri. In 1899, he spoke at the Woman's Progressive Union in New York. His lectures included: "Heaven: What, Where and Who's There" and "The Scope and Value of the Spiritualist Platform."

For 30 years, Frank was a lecturer, singer and medium. He was also a member of the Temple Heights Spiritualist Corporation of Northport for many years. He died in February 1904 from typhoid fever at the age of 62.

BISHOP A. BEALS

Bishop Beals born in 1832 in Versailles, New York to Amplius and Olive Beals. His father was a physician, and he and his family were members of the Universalist church. In 1856, when living in New York City, Bishop joined the congregation of Rev. E. H. Chapin and became interested in Spiritualism. He attended a demonstration by 14-year-old medium, Miss Libbie Lowe, and was struck with wonder. He said that she woke the latent power of mediumship within him.

Bishop served in the New York Infantry during the Civil War and was discharged due to a disability in 1861. It wasn't until after the death of his mother in 1865, that he began a career as a public teacher and speaker. He worked as a trance speaker, poet, singer, and musician.

In an interview for the *Carrier Dove*, vol. 3 no. 10, October 1886, Bishop stated, "I do not recollect a time that I was not visited with strange, prophetic dreams and trance-like visions. I have always been conscious of the nearness of the spiritual world. I was, even in childhood, a worshipper at the shrine of nature, and later in life I found her sweet influences far more in harmony with my religious aspirations than were the religious doctrines of popular churches."

Mrs. C. H. Decker Buchanan said that Bishop was sensitive and preferred to let "his works praise themselves. The circling waves of harmony surround his efforts; his resolves spring from the purest motives, and when understood must endear him to all who are associated with him socially."

During the mid-1870s through the 1890s, Bishop traveled through New York and New England, across the Midwest, including Kansas, Missouri and Illinois, and then went west to California, where he spoke in Santa Barbara, Stockton, and San Francisco. His lectures included: "The World's True Redeemer," "The Evolution of Thought," "New Dispensation," and "What is Truth?" His lectures were often accompanied by music, song and his own poetry.

Bishop moved to Oakland, California in the 1880s and married late in life to Eliza Cone in 1895. *The Waterloo Press*, 7 March 1895, described him as one of many curious people. "...this professor, who is of ordinary stature with long (will-be-silver) locks of hair swinging to and fro about his head attracting the attention of everybody, made his appearance in this city last week." It continued, "He compared men of today with those of from one hundred to five hundred years ago and said that men are now governed by laws of mercy."

After living in California for two decades, Bishop returned to his home state of New York. He died in 1909 while living in the Lily Dale area.

Olive A. Blodgett

Olive A Blodgett was born in New Hampshire about 1840. She married Joseph C. Blodgett and by 1860 they were living in Columbia, Wisconsin where Joseph worked as a farmer. They would later move to Davenport, Iowa. Olive was listed as a slate-writing medium, presenting communications from H. M. Hoxie at one of The Mississippi Valley Spiritualist Association seances in April 1887. Joseph was a traveling salesman at the time. Olive was later listed as a physician in the Davenport 1890 directory.

Both Joseph and Olive were involved with Spiritualism. In 1871, they held a birthday dinner in honor of Will C. Hodges. *The Progressive Thinker* vol. 3 no. 67, 7 March 1871, wrote, "Spirit 'Pansy' took control of her medium, Mrs. Ollie A. Blodgett, and recited a beautiful poem entitled 'The Message of the Flowers.'"

At a meeting in Dubuque, the *Sioux City Journal*, 5 April 1892, reported "…platform tests by Mrs. Blodgett, a trance medium, of Davenport, through whose entranced brain 'Bright Eyes,' an Indian girl spoke, asking and receiving from the audience recognition of many who had 'passed out' to the spirit land."

Olive wrote a Letter to Editor of *The Progressive Thinker*, vol. 6 no. 157, 26 Nov 1892, and said, "Your paper is most excellent and a general favorite. About the holidays I intend to do some missionary work in sending out a few yearly subscriptions of *The Progressive Thinker*, for I count each day lost in which I have done no good or made nobody happy. We have got to be unselfish, charitable and kind; and our work must be practicable and our relations to the human family must be to do good everywhere we see it should be done; for, as you say, we cannot receive the highest spiritual teachings and do nothing."

Olive was involved with the Ladies Independent Union which helped care for Mt. Pleasant Park, the local Spiritualist camp. She was also Vice President and on the board of directors of the Mississippi Valley Spiritualists Association in 1890, and a national delegate in 1893 and 1894. In October 1894, Olive said the Invocation and Cora V. L. Richmond the dedication for the new headquarters of the National Spiritualist Association in Washington, D.C.

Olive was still a prominent member of the Mississippi Valley Spiritualists association at the time of her death in 1894. In her will, she left her husband her property in the spiritualist community, Summerland, California, as well as in Tacoma, Washington. The *Quad-City Times* (Davenport, IA), 16 December 1894 reported, "The husband is requested to provide for the cremation of the wife's body and the scattering of her ashes to the four winds, and thereafter to arrange for a memorial service at such time and place as will result in the most good to humanity."

HELEN TEMPLE BRIGHAM

Helen (Nellie) Temple was born in 1843 in Manchester, Vermont, the fourth child of Jabez and Mary Temple. Her first spiritual demonstration was held in Glens Falls, New York in the old Universalists church when she was 14 years old. By the age of 16, she was listed in the census as a Spiritual Medium living with her parents in Whittingham, Vermont. The family moved to Colrain, Massachusetts and she began her public speaking career at the age of 18.

Helen was well-known by 1861 and was listed in many Spiritualist publications. She married farmer, Luther A. Brigham in 1865 and had a son a year later, but that did not slow her down. She continued with her public speaking, appearing in various places through the 1870s-1890s in New England and New York.

Helen's husband died in August of 1895 at the age of 60. Helen continued with her public speaking. In 1896, she was a guest at the Psychical Hall, reciting impromptu poems chosen by the audience. According to the *Post Star*, Glens Falls, New York, "The public are respectfully invited to witness these wonderful phenomena of the voicings of the angel world."

Helen moved to New York City where she lodged with Belle V. Cushman, president of the Spiritual and Ethical Society of New York. In 1896, they sailed from New York to England and traveled around Europe for 6 months. She became friends with Sir Oliver Lodge and Sir Arthur Conan Doyle.

In 1897, Helen continued with her impromptu public poetry, composing works such as "No Night There," "The Choir in Our Village," "Lake George," and "How It Ended." In 1899 at Glens Falls, she spoke on a variety of subjects, including "Why Does God Allow Evil to Predominate in the World?" and What is Heaven Like?" Her poems included: "Fall Blossoms," "Spirit Guidance," and "Father, Brother and Sisters in the Spirit Land"

Helen's appearances continued through the early 1900s. In 1901, she was a speaker at Queen City Park Spiritualists Camp in Burlington, Vermont. In 1902 she traveled to Australia and New Zealand. The *Topeka Daily Capital,* 3 October 1909, reported on the Convention of the Society for Scientific Revelation at the Temple of Health in Kansas City, Missouri. They wrote, "Another lecturer and teacher, whose beautiful lessons have been given in all parts of the world, Mrs. Helen Temple Brigham, of New York City, will also be present. Mrs. Brigham has just returned from a lecturing tour through Europe and Australia. She has been pastor of one church or society in New York City for more than 40 years. Her lectures are uplifting and filled with words of wisdom which brings her close to the heart of her audience the very moment she begins to talk. God has gifted but a few with such powers of description and inspiration, as is possessed by Mrs. Helen Temple Brigham."

Helen passed on to the spirit world in 1923. The *North Adams Transcript,* 17 February 1923, wrote, "Mrs. Brigham was always ready to give her hometown the best of her ability and had preached from every pulpit in the town, lectured for the benefit of various organizations and the hospitality of her home was famous. A woman of charming personality, Christian character and beloved by all who knew her, she was for fifty years the pastor of the Spiritual and Ethical society in New York. During this time, she spent most of her summers at her home here. Mrs. Brigham had traveled extensively from Canada to Mexico and in foreign countries. She had lectured in England, Ireland, Scotland and Wales."

GEORGE H. BROOKS

George H. Brooks was born in 1853 to Anson and Polly Brooks in Adams, New York. By 1870 he was living in Chicago, and in the early 1880s in Madison, Wisconsin. He married Frances Elizabeth Short from Dane, Wisconsin in 1883 and worked as a Spiritualist lecturer and medium.

During the 1880s, George was listed as a medium at Lamar House, Knoxville, Tennessee, giving private readings for $1 an hour. He also worked in Topeka, Kansas, Lily Dale and Cassadaga. The *Wheeling Sunday Register*, 17 March 1889, posted, "G. H. Brooks, trance medium, will lecture in G. A. R. Hall today, morning at 10:30 and 7:30 o'clock in the evening. Subjects taken from the audience. Private sittings daily at No. 74 Fourteenth street."

The Progressive Thinker, Vol. 4 No. 104, 21 November 1891, published *Notes from G.H. Brooks,* which discussed starting meetings in Elgin, Illinois. He wrote, "In my last letter I was unsettled, and knew nothing of the spiritual condition of this city. As soon as I could I started out, and soon found a number of warm friends to our cause. All speak in the highest terms of THE PROGRESSIVE THINKER. The friends were very anxious for me to start meetings here, believing it a good field. There had been no public work here, aside from what Prof. Lockwood and his wife had done in the summer, for years; so, after thinking over the matter, I finally consented. There was a much larger audience the first Sunday than I expected, and the meetings have increased in numbers and interest, until I trust that out of this there will come forth a strong spiritual society."

George was active in Spiritualism during the 1890s. He was the chairman of Haslet Park, a Spiritualist camp, for six years, lecturing and doing psychometer readings. He was also a Michigan State missionary, street chairman at Lily Dale, and a member of the Conference of National Spiritualists. At the Fort Wayne First Spiritual Society, one of his lectures was entitled: "The Moral Influence of Spiritualism."

George and his wife had one son, born in 1903, before they moved to Los Angeles by 1910. He continued his work as a traveling lecturer. As a renowned minister, Doctor of Divinity & lecturer from Los Angeles, he also held seminars in the Cottonwood, Arizona area regularly.

It was April 20, 1925. George was staying at the Cottonwood Hotel which he did frequently. The town of Cottonwood paid a large sum to bring him into town. At that visit, it is said that he predicted his death while giving psychic readings. At 3:00 am, a still located in the rear of the Thomas Moore Restaurant blew up. The fire it created was fanned by a strong wind that swept along the two blocks of the westside of Main St. Fifteen businesses and 10 residential homes were destroyed. The Cottonwood Hotel, a wooden structure, also caught fire.

The only town fatality was Reverend Brooks. It appeared that George had been awakened by the fire, partially dressed himself, and fell, overcome by the heat and smoke. His body was buried in Inglewood, California. Some say he still walks around the hotel in the upper hallway.

Mercy E. Cadwallader

In the 1890s, Mercy Cadwallader lived in Philadelphia where she worked for the Oriental Publishing Company. She was involved with the publishing of *Antiquity Unveiled* by J. M. Roberts. It was here that Mercy became interested in Spiritualism. She joined the National Spiritualist Association (NSA) which was organized in 1893, and in 1894 she was elected honorary Vice-President.

After moving to Chicago, Mercy entertained prominent Spiritualists from all over the world and was a strong proponent of the religion. She became editor of *The Progressive Thinker*, which she purchased in 1910 after the death of its founder J. R. Francis. She was also known for her interest in the Fox Family and their remarkable story. She wrote *Hydesville in History* (1917), published by The Progressive Thinker Publishing House.

Mercy was also a member of the Chicago Spiritualists' League. In 1917 she held the position of Vice-President. Mediums of the league were vigorously tested by a board of trustees and certificated if they achieved the required mediumistic standards. This level of training not only assured the quality of mediums, it stood up in the court of law.

Mercy was called to testify on behalf of Spiritualism. Mrs. Minnie Parsons was being accused of fortunetelling for money which was in violation of the laws of the State of Illinois. The judge needed to determine if the Chicago Spiritualists' League was a bona fide corporation, and that Minnie Parsons was a member.

Mercy testified about the religion of Spiritualism, its history, the NSA, and their training requirements for mediums. The judge asked about private readings and public demonstrations. Mercy explained that both were practiced. He was concerned that the police were unable to determine true mediums from charlatans. Mercy promised to help authorities determine which mediums were imposters. Mrs. Parsons was discharged because of her membership and certification in the league.

In another court case, Mrs. Charlotte Longstaff, a certified medium of the Chicago Spiritualists' League, was also tried on a charge of fortunetelling. The judge stated that under the law, spirit mediums had a right to practice their gifts because the law was not intended to interfere with religion.

Mercy was particularly interested in education and played a prominent role in building the Andrew Jackson Davis Lyceum building in 1928 at Lily Dale, New York. The children's playground is known as Cadwallader Park. She also traveled to England and was welcomed by like-minded Spiritualists across the country.

Mercy continued working until the 1930s. In 1934, after a long illness, she passed on to the Spirit World.

DR. DEAN CLARKE (CLARK)

Dean Clark was born in Royalton, Vermont in 1837 to Jedediah and Mary Clark. He helped his father on their farm and was still working there in 1860 at the age of 23. Dean married Harriet Horton Bardy in 1863 in Sudbury, Vermont where he worked as a physician. It is unclear what happened to Harriet. By 1870, Dean was traveling the country as a Spiritualist lecturer.

Dean lived in several communities, from Chicago, Illinois to Oakland and San Francisco, California, to Portland, Oregon between 1872 and 1886. He returned to the Boston area in 1887, but still travelled widely. He was speaker at the Liberal Spiritualist Society in Oakland at their 44th anniversary celebration in 1892. In 1900 he was a representative of the American National Spiritualist Association at the Paris Congress and visited London while abroad.

A Guide to Mediumship and Psychical Unfoldment by E. W. and M. H. Wallis contained several quotes from Dean dealing with mediumship, magnetism, and physical phenomena. One from the *Banner of Light* stated: "The word mediumship, as understood and used by Spiritualists, technically speaking, means a susceptibility to the influence, and more or less control, of decarnated spirits. Physiologically, it means a peculiar nervous susceptibility to what may be termed the 'psychic force,' which spirits use to move the mind or body, or both, of their moral instrument." He added that, "Novices in mediumship have no business to assume obligations they are not fully qualified to fulfill."

In the *Progressive Thinker,* vol. 2 no. 36, 2 August 1890, he wrote "Our work is that of pioneers. Let us do it faithfully and well, carrying our standard in the vein, bearing the motto: 'Spiritualism Pure and Simple, Unalloyed by Theosophic Speculations.'"

Dean was living with his brother and family in Brookline, Massachusetts in 1910. He died two years later, in September of 1912 and was buried near his hometown in Vermont.

LUCIUS COLBURN

Lucius Colburn was born in Plymouth, Vermont in 1854 to Moses and Eunice Colburn. He had a younger brother who died in 1879 while they lived near Rutland. Lucius never married and devoted himself to lecturing and working as a medium the rest of his life.

During the 1880s and 1890s, Lucius traveled throughout Vermont while living in Manchester. He gave lecturers, inspirational speeches, sermons, improvised poetry, and readings in Orleans County, Essex Junction, St. Albans, East Wallingford, South Barre, Tyson, and Reading.

Lucius was a member of the Vermont Spiritualist Association and participated in most of their meetings as lecturer and medium. At the 1890 spiritual convention in Tyson, he gave the opening address, had a séance in a closed session, gave a lecture, improvised a poem and sang music to close the day's meeting. He also attended Spiritualist Camps, like Lake Sunapee (New Hampshire) in 1885 where he was known for his "satisfactory tests as a medium."

The Spiritualists of Lawrence County, New York held a convention at West Potsdam in 1892 where Lucius was the leading speaker. The following year, the *Progressive Thinker,* vol. 7 no. 184, 3 June 1893, wrote that "Bro. Lucius Colburn is kept very busy going from one part of the state (Vermont) to another, holding meetings and test circles. In his circles he had convinced many a doubting Thomas of spirit return." By the late 1890s, Lucius was referred to as reverend and conducted sermons in Orleans County on Sundays.

In the 1900 census, Lucius R. Colburn referred to himself as a clergyman. At the 1903 Vermont state convention, Lucius gave a talk entitled, "Is Life worth Living?" It was sometime after that that he moved to California. Reporting on the Summerland Camp Meeting in the *Progressive Thinker*, vol. 5 no. 210, 10 October 1914, John T. Lillie wrote, "Lucius Colburn eloquent, earnest and honest, not only in his rostrum work helped the camp, but by labor in the entertainments and by contributions did much to make the meeting a financial success."

Around 1910, Lucius started the Vermont Society in Santa Barbara, California and was President. At the same time, he attended the state Spiritualists association in Los Angeles and gave Impromptu poems. He was a 1912 San Diego convention speaker. In 1913 he was listed as Mr. Lucius Colburn, pastor of the Progressive Church in Pasadena.

In the *Press-Telegram*, 10 Nov 1913, they wrote of Lucius, "Speaking on the 'the ideal life' at the First Spiritualist church, Universal temple, 415 Linden avenue, Lucius Colburn, of Pasadena said: "We are living today in a most remarkable age. The religions of the past have been of the material nature instead of the spiritual. Our ideals are the real life. Whoever lives to manifest in this life manifests his ideal—it is not the life beyond, but the life onward. The inmost thought of the soul has yet to be expressed and we must begin with child life to develop it. Colburn said while we are chiseling or developing or characters let us strive to make for the very highest ideals we can conceive, Let us do it now, and not wait for some time to come. Let us with our own deeds, actions and principles work out all life's problems and success and an ideal life will be ours."

In the 1910s, Lucius owned a boarding house, was a member of the Green Mountain Club, and attended Mineral Park Spiritualist camp. He continued with his Spiritualist lectures in California but died a tragic death in 1925. As a boarding house owner, he was known to have plenty of money on him all the time. Thieves broke into his room and tied and gagged him. He did not survive the attack.

GEORGE P. COLBY

George P. Colby was born in the state of New York in 1848, but moved to Forestville Township, Minnesota when he was a child where he lived on a farm with his devout Baptist family. Shortly after his baptism, at the age of twelve, George was visited by the spirit of his uncle. His uncle told him he had great psychic ability and would found a spiritual center in the South.

Heeding his uncle's advice, George developed his mediumship skills during his teen years, practicing trance clairvoyance, spiritual readings, and healing. He was regularly punished and beaten by his parents for his actions until he left his home and church in 1867.

George became a traveling medium, conducting private readings and parlor séances. He worked with several spirit guides including a Native American named Seneca. It was Seneca who told him to visit Theodore D. Giddings in Eau Claire, Wisconsin. The spirit then instructed the two of them to find land in Florida on which to build a spiritualist center.

George purchased land, built a house and farmed the new property which he called Southern Cassadaga. In 1893, Dr. William Rowley opened a winter camp for spiritualists in De Leon Springs, Florida. His group, The National Spiritual and Liberal Association, outgrew their original location. Emma Huff convinced them that part of George's property would make an ideal camp. Under the direction of Thomas and Marion Skidmore, Abbie Pettengill, Emma Huff and others, they obtained the property and created the Southern Cassadaga Spiritualist Camp Meeting Association in 1894. George offered the use of his home for the grand opening, was elected its first President, and worked at the camp as medium and orator.

After many years traveling as a medium, lecturer and spiritualist leader, George's health began to deteriorate. The Florida climate renewed him for a time, but it did not last. In 1933, at the age of 85, George was forced to give up his travels. He was provided with a place to live at the camp, and the members saw to his needs until his death in July of that year.

After George's passing, Cassadaga encountered resistance from local Baptist churches, but during the 1960s enjoyed increasing popularity because of New Age influences. Today, the camp consists of approximately fifty-five homes located on over fifty-seven acres.

Cassadaga is the nation's only year-round Spiritualist community. Many of its 200 residents are mediums and healers. The town looks much as it did a century ago, with cottages lining the tree-shaded streets. Guests may stay at the Cassadaga Hotel built in 1927 and visit the central auditorium, Colby Memorial Temple erected in 1923, community library, Andrew Jackson Davis Educational building, Caesar Forman Healing Center, Camp Bookstore, and welcome center. The Camp was designated a Historic District and placed on the National Register of Historic Places in 1991.

LUTHER COLBY

Luther Colby was born in 1814 to Captain William and Mary Colby in Amesbury, Massachusetts. He attended common schools in the area and at the age of 15 became a printers' apprentice in Exeter, New Hampshire. His first important work was type setting an edition of *Scott's Family Bible and the New Testament* with another apprentice.

In 1836, Luther moved to Boston where he worked for the *Boston Daily Post*, one of the city's leading newspapers. He remained there for twenty years, working his way up to the editorial room. By that time Luther was a materialist and had no interest in any kind of religion. When Spiritualism began to grow in the 1850s, he first ignored it.

Some of those in Massachusetts who were interested in Spiritualism included: Dr. Henry F Gardner, Rev. Allen Putnam, Mrs. A. E. Newton, and William Berry. It was through fellow printer, Mr. Berry, that Luther was introduced to seances. At an initial seance at the residence of Mrs. Sterns, Luther first met Mrs. J. H. Conant. He was so impressed with her that he recommended Mr. Berry invite her to hold a series of weekly seances at his home.

Mr. Berry was told by the spirit world through Mrs. Conant in 1856 that he would change jobs and publish a paper to be called *Banner of Light*. And Luther was right there with all the right publishing experience to help him. The two founded and edited the *Banner of Light* in Boston beginning in 1857. It became the longest running publication of its kind in the nineteenth century.

Luther was not a prominent man nor book author, but he firmly believed that truth could best be served by a careful publication of all alleged communications from the "sphere of light" to the "mortal state."

He was convinced that the revelations of Spiritualism published by the *Banner of Light* would revolutionize the world. It was his policy that "we shall not believe everything but shall not refuse to listen to what is said." After Mr. Berry was killed in the Civil War, Luther continued to serve as editor until his death in 1894.

In a memorial address Lyman C. Howe said, "He has come to touch with millions through his public ministrations, with thousands personally; and every one who has felt the life of his touch retains the impress of his individuality still. That impress is, and will continue to be, a modifying influence in the direction of character and its development. He was strong in convictions, and ready to carry out, according to his best understanding, the highest ideals of his life; and in his departure we shall miss all these outward, tangible expressions, and none can take his place from this time, though others, perhaps, are equally as well qualified to give direction to the work …."

WILLIAM J. COLVILLE

William J. Colville was born about 1859 in England. Little is known about his early life. His mother died when he was a boy. His father lived only a few years after her death. From a young age William "expressed certain traits peculiar to highly sensitive organisms; and though he and others may have been spiritually unconscious of what was working beneath the surface, yet indications of some occult force were at times unmistakable," according to an article in *Medium and Daybreak,* Vol 9, No 442, Sept 20, 1878.

William was brought up in an orthodox church and first felt his talent was the work of the devil, but he overcame that fear. When he was 17, he attended a lecture by Mrs. Cora L.V. Tappan in 1874. Inspired, he returned home and composed a poem "The Resurrection." He began to occasionally read his inspirational poetry, received while in a trance state, in private homes.

By the time he was 19, William was able to "deliver discourses with the same fluency as at the present time. The special phase of his mediumship, which is inspirational speaking, is about to undergo a great change." After that, physical phenomenon, rapping, table oscillations took place. He had 12 guides who communicated through him for public demonstrations, including Native American spirits.

In September of 1878, he addressed a select meeting at the Spiritual Institution in London before leaving for the United States. He made his home in Boston for the next decade. He was a popular speaker in the city and at Spiritualist camps. He attended Queen City Park in Burlington, Vermont and Lookout Mountain in Tennessee, and was a regular guest at Lily Dale in New York. At the 1888 Tenth Anniversary of American Spiritualism lectures in Boston, he made his farewell appearance before traveling to California.

Between lectures, William also published several articles, books and edited journals. His books included: *The Spiritual Science of Health and Healing* (1887), *Universal Theosophy: The Science of Health and Healing* (1887), *Spiritual Therapeutics; or, Divine Science,* (1888), *A History of Theosophy* (1896), and *Old and New Psychology* (1897).

While in California, William lectured, taught classes, and was the manager for George Chainey and Anna Kimballâ's *Gnostic* in San Francisco. He then published an edited *The Problem of Life* (1890-1893) with Alzire A. Chevailler. The publication was, "Devoted to Spiritual Science and Philosophy and all Subjects Pertaining to the Welfare and Progress of Humanity / A Magazine Devoted to Spiritual Science and Philosophy as related to Universal Human Progress."

In his first issue, he wrote, "How many are there who enter the ranks as teachers and practitioners of Spiritual, Mental, or Christian Science, who realize anything more than a very small part of the work they are called upon to do, and how many are there who even attempt to begin at what is really the right end of the line, if true progress is to be made? The moral elevation of the race is of primary importance, its intellectual advancement is of secondary value, its physical soundness comes third."

William returned to London in 1914 and gave lectures to the London Spiritualist Alliance and The Buddhist Society of Great Britain and Ireland. During his life, he toured the U.S., England and Australia. He died in San Francisco in January of 1917. His obituary stated that, "W. J. Colville, one of the foremost British lecturers on theosophical topics, died yesterday at the Wiltshire apartments after a brief illness with pneumonia." He was 57 years old and "spent many years lecturing and writing."

JOHN W. DAY

John W. Day was born in Gloucester, Massachusetts in 1838, son of Joseph and Augusta Day. His maternal grandfather was Rev. Ezra Leonard, a convert to Universalism. John was educated in grammar schools and went to high school in Portsmouth at the Hampton Academy. He joined the office of *The Trumpet*, a Universalist publication, and then the *Banner of Light* soon after its inception in 1857 as an apprentice to "the art preservative."

He thought of joining the Universalist ministry but his poor eyesight, which made him abandon printing as well, lead to several outdoor jobs. He spent 2 years at sea and 5 years in the army, ending as a captain in the cavalry from 1861-1866. When he returned to Boston in 1867, he worked for *The Banner of Light* as compositor, shorthand reporter, and associate editor. In 1880, he married Nellie M. King, twenty years his junior, of Cambridge, Massachusetts. He was a member of the Masons, Odd Fellows, and the Grand Army of the Republic.

In 1880, he was living with the King family and working as reporter at age 42; Nellie was 23 and they had no children. John authored many poems and recited them at Spiritualist meetings in the Boston area. Twenty of the poems were published as *A Galaxy of Progressive Poems* in Boston in 1890.

His "The Wine of the Spirit" begins:

> Another year hath trod th' arena's floor
>
> Where uses stern to Being's call respond;
>
> And we with gladness hail the loved once more
>
> Who bring their message from the Fair Beyond!

We mark with joy Progression's prophet shine

That streams puissant from that primal ray

When angel fingers from the land divine

Swept the dark lignite clouds of doubt away.

According to the *Biography of Mrs. J.H. Conant, the World's Medium of the Nineteenth Century,* published in 1873, "Mr. John W. Day, a reporter at the Banner of Light office, listened on many occasions to utterances through Mrs. Conant while she was under control by Parker (spirit Theodore Parker), and minuted in shorthand what that spirit desired to put forth as a biography of his medium."

Unfortunately, John died from a gunshot wound in Somerville, Massachusetts in 1898 after he retired from working at the *Banner of Light.* His work as editor and reporter greatly influenced the dissemination of information about Spiritualism across the country.

JOSEPH W. DENNIS

Joseph W. Dennis was born in 1827 in Green County, New York to Joseph and Julia Ann Dennis. He married Delia Toles, and they had two children before she died. He married his second wife, Lucy Mayfield, in the late 1850s and they had a son in 1860. Joseph lived in Buffalo most of his life, working as a dock builder and contractor. In was reported in his obituary that he built most of the docks and coal trestles in the city of Buffalo. He was prominent in Republican politics and was an alderman during 1873-1874 for the third ward.

It is unclear when Joseph became involved in Spiritualism. He posted an advertisement in *The Watchman* in 1887. It said, "Send to J. W. Dennis for a sheet of his Magnetized Paper which is a magnet that will bring to the wearer, a Spirit Guide for Development or Healing. Ten cents per sheet. Can give references from mediums."

The Buffalo News, 14 March, 1895, published one of Joseph's poems submitted by another person. "J.W. Dennis, who wrote the verses quoted, is a Buffalo man, well known in Lily Dale, and every spiritualist in Buffalo will laugh over this satire on Mr. Dennis. His request to not mourn for him appeared in the *Progressive Thinker*, March 6, 1895.

When I am Born Again

No black for me
No robes of night,
  No clouded brow,
But robes of light;
  No pall on coffin lid,
No priestly quack
  No tears of grief,
No hireling hack,

No woes, no wails,
No sorrow's veins.
But shouts of joy
    And songs of mirth
Proclaim the news,
    "Another birth."

Joseph was a member of the Buffalo Spiritual Church Society and gave many lectures at their meetings in the late 1890s. In a 1900 announcement, he was referred to as reverend. He gave the lectures alongside medium Mrs. C Lewis Chase, who gave readings. In 1903, Joseph attended Lily Dale with prominent Spiritualists, Carrie E. S. Twing, W. M. Lockwood, and W. J. Hull. He was a regular contributor to the *Harmonia,* published in 1885-1886, and published a piece called "My Vision" in the January 1886, vol. 1 no. 7 issue.

Joseph's wife, Lucy, died in 1911. He followed the next year at the age of 85. City hall flags flew at half-mast on the day of his funeral in his honor.

EDWARD HANIGAN DENSLOW

Edward Hanigan Denslow was born in 1844 in Mount Pleasant, Indiana to farmers Henry and Sarah Denslow. In his younger days he spent time traveling with the circus and theatrical companies in the west. He took up drinking but was "transformed" after marrying his first wife, Anna S. Johnson, in 1865, and having three children. In 1873, he discovered that he possessed healing powers and opened an office in South Bend where he used laying-on of hands to ease and cure ailments. He later opened a sanitarium in Sturgis, Michigan.

The *South Bend Tribune*, 27 November 1880, published a statement from Edward: "Since the publication of my Thanksgiving proclamation, I find that the question is often asked, how is it possible that the so-called magnetic and motorpathic healing can in any way produce beneficial effects upon diseased organizations? Without entering into a discussion of the subject here, I invite all interested in the matter to call at my office over Strayer's gun store on Michigan Street and I will convince you there is nothing impossible or mysterious about it."

The 1880s came with terrible losses for Edward. His brother, Robert, passed in 1884. Anna, his first wife, died in 1885. He then lost their daughter Cora to illness in 1886. By that time, Edward was a well-known magnetic physician in South Bend. He eventually married Clara Balfour of Bangor, Michigan in South Bend, Indiana in 1887, the same year his daughter Grace married. By 1890, he had moved his office to Sturgis, Michigan.

In the late 1880s, Edward became a missionary for the National Spiritualist Association. He traveled west to Wichita and Kansas City. In 1897, at the First Society of Spiritualists, Kansas City, he was a guest trance speaker.

The Kansas City Journal, 22 February 1897, wrote, "The subject of the address was the transference of thought on waves of ether. Dr. Denslow took the position that every wave of ether bore some one or more thoughts emanating from either the physical or spiritual world. He believed there was a tendency toward the refinement of ether and to increased sensitiveness on the part of the people, so that impressions derived from ether waves were more frequent and distinct than formerly." He was quoted as saying: "I have never known a bad spirit. The spirits who seek to communicate with us are good spirits. Their influences are for the good, and by making ourselves susceptible to the thought transference received through the action of the ether we can place ourselves in communication with the natures which will exert upon us the best influences and neutralize the tendency to bad of the physical world."

The *Fort Wayne Sentinel*, 6 Nov 1901, wrote, "Mr. Denslow is a highly developed medium and his life readings are of a high order of excellence and very satisfactory. Advice given upon all questions pertaining to the welfare of mankind."

Edward, along with his second wife, Clara, and her sister died in a tragic fire in 1906. Clara, who had suffered with depression, decided to take her own life by dousing herself and then her husband with gasoline in their home. The resulting fire led to their deaths. Edward was 62 and along with being a popular healer, was remembered for his membership in the Masons and the Knights Templar of Sturgis.

MAUD LORD-DRAKE

Maud E. Barrock was born in 1852 in Marion County, West Virginia, the fourth child of Sarah J. and Phillip S. Barrock. They said she was born with a double veil over her face. When she was only a toddler, luminous lights were sometimes seen about her, and sparks flew from her hair. She liked to spend time in the dark and often her mother couldn't find her. Her cradle rocked by itself. By the age of five, she had unseen playmates and said she could hear the trees and plants singing. Of course, her parents didn't take kindly to all these happenings and thought the devil was behind everything.

A kettle of boiling lye accidentally spilled on Maud when she was a child, and she was treated by a doctor. When the doctor returned to the house, she asked for pencil and paper and wrote, "Get pine needles, crush and mix with linseed oil, put between beet leaves and apply immediately." The doctor recognized an old friend's handwriting and did as he was instructed. Maud recovered.

Her parents refused to educate her, believing her abilities were the work of the devil. She tried to sneak off to school but was caught. Finally, during a moment of temporary blindness, a spirit came to her and instructed her on how she would learn from the spirit world in a grove of trees near the creek. And that she did.

When the Civil War began, the family moved to Iowa. Maud spoke French and German by then, advised neighbors about the war, and found missing things. She also communicated with spirits via rapping sounds. Her parents still rejected her abilities. Maud ran away at one point but returned home where her parents took her to church for an exorcism. She ran away again, and even thought of suicide before finding

Mr. John J. Hall from New York City. He told her she was a medium. Her spirit guide came to her then. His name was Clarence.

In 1868, Maud married Albert Lord in Wisconsin. They had one daughter who was known as Adrienne de Corische. After Albert died, Maud married J. S. Drake in 1887. He was a contractor and hydraulic engineer, was involved with politics, and was also a newspaper writer. "Mr. Drake apparently has the ability, education, experience, courage and inclination so necessary to assist in this important work," according to *The Religio-Philosophical Journal*, 1887.

In 1900, they were living in St. Louis. Drake was listed as a lawyer and she a lecturer. He was ten years her senior. They eventually moved to Boulder Creek, California where they lived 27 years. After Drake died in about 1914, an Ernst Lydick from Pittsburgh received many spiritual messages from Maud's control, Clarence, and her deceased husband to travel to California and take care of her.

Maud and Ernst were eventually married. She initially survived burns when her house burned at Boulder Creek but died in 1924 in Santa Cruz. According to her biography, "For many years a spiritualist of considerable prominence, the events of the wedded life of the deceased woman, as told this morning by her third husband, Ernst B. Lydick, also a spiritualist and author of various literary works of psychic phenomena form an unusual and sometimes weird story."

Maud's biography was published as *Psychic Light: The Continuity of Law and Life* in 1904 by Frank T. Riley Publishing Co. Kansas City, Missouri and contains much more information about her.

OSCAR A. EDGERLY

Oscar Edgerly was born in New York state in 1863 to Samuel and Lucy Edgerly. His family moved to New Hampshire when he was only 6 years old, and his father worked as a farmer. By 1880, the family was living in Newburyport, Massachusetts. Oscar was 16 and worked at a cotton mill. By 1886, the 23-year-old was a boarder working in Newburyport.

At the age of 25, Oscar was already attending Spiritualist meetings. In 1888, he spoke to the Spiritual Phenomena Association in Boston. That led to engagements at Camp Onset and in Minnesota where he lectured in St Paul and Minneapolis speaking about such topics as "Spiritualism as a Religion," and "Selfishness, the Bane of our Age." The *Saint Paul Globe*, 6 April 1895, referred to Oscar as "… one of the leading spiritual mediums and lecturers in the country, delivered a lecture, and the service ended with a test circle."

The *Lewiston Daily Sun* (Lewiston, Maine), 6 February 1895, published news from Anderson, Indiana, saying that "Oscar Edgerly, the Spiritualist lecturer of Newburyport, Mass., was married in this city last night to Miss Lillian Hayes of St. Paul, daughter of the general superintendent of the Great Northern, and a leading society lady of that city." It added that "The groom is a noted spiritualist lecturer and has an engagement of a month in this city (Anderson)."

There is no indication that Lillian participated in Spiritualism while Oscar's lectures took him around the country to cities such as Atlanta; Boston; Covington, Kentucky; and Minneapolis. By 1905, Lillian filed for divorce, due to "his drinking and willful absence for three years."

Oscar continued his speaking tour, traveling to Lily Dale and Camp Chesterfield; Deland, Florida; and Los Angeles, where he met his second wife. He married Florence Robson, an established medium, in 1912.

They advertised in the Los Angeles paper as mediums who gave daily readings and traveled together to camps Lily Dale, Temple Heights, and Grand Ledge.

The *Houston Post*, 23 December 1912, reported on a lecture Oscar delivered as acting pastor of the First Spiritualist Society of Houston. The paper ran a long article on his lecture which included the following, "The world does move, and the Twentieth Century must attest to the fact in the revealments of science in every department of human observation and experience. Mediumship is of the spirit—it is innate; it cannot be imparted to a human being by any other, though sometimes it can be assisted in its growth by the magnetism and sympathy of some good and sensitive friend on the other side of life. Mediumship is dependent on rates of vibration for its quality of manifestation. Its relations are to the perception, and its mental phases of expression can only become active by the quickening of the spiritual perception of the sensitive."

Oscar and Florence toured Texas together during April 1913, and attended the Los Angeles convention in 1915 where Oscar spoke on "Spiritualism Considered as a Science, Religion and Philosophy," and appeared at the Burbank People's Spiritualist Church lecture. By 1916, Oscar was referred to as reverend and was giving readings and lectures at the Spiritualist Church of Revelation.

Oscar's second marriage did not last. In 1916, Florence filed for divorce for non-support and his drinking. Oscar continued to give messages, and his travels took him to Lima, Ohio; Chicago; Lily Dale; Lansing, Michigan; Camp Chesterfield; and Cassadaga, Florida.

At the end of his life, Oscar was single, a member of the Daytona Florida Elks Lodge and lived at the Elks Hotel Home. Oscar died in Florida in 1929 and was buried by his brother in Bedford, Virginia.

EDGAR W. EMERSON

Edgar W. Emerson was born in Boscawen, New Hampshire about 1855 to Francis and Julia Emerson. Edgar was the fourth of six children born to the couple. His father worked in cotton and sawmills and Edgar joined him as a mill worker when he was 16. He later worked as a carpenter.

By 1880, Edgar's father had passed, and Edgar was living at home in Manchester, New Hampshire with his older brother, Charles, their mother and his 11-year-old twin siblings, Julius and Julia. Charles was listed as a painter in the census and Edgar as a "Spiritualist MD." He travelled extensively over the next three decades, working as both a lecturer and medium at many of the camps in the northeastern United States, including Lily Dale, Lake Pleasant, Sunapee, Hazlet Park, and Neshaminy Falls. He was a welcome guest to Spiritualist groups in Brooklyn, Boston, Buffalo, Pittsburgh, Cincinnati and Indianapolis.

The Buffalo Courier, 27 August 1890, wrote: "The day's entertainments were closed with some remarkable platform tests, by Edgar W. Emerson of Manchester, N. H. Some 20 different tests were given to persons located in various places in the auditorium. It is hardly presumable that by any collusion the medium would be able to locate all of these persons in scattered positions. The names of deceased friends were given, with time and cause of death, residence, personal description, etc. Besides all this, the persons to whom the tests were given were pointed out."

By 1900, Edgar was listed in the census as a clairvoyant living with his twin siblings. There is no indication that he ever married. *The Greenfield Recorder* (Massachusetts), 21 September 1904, wrote, "Edgar W. Emerson, whose powers as a psychic and test medium have attracted the attention of scientists and scholars far and near, will lecture and give messages at the meeting of the Greenfield Spiritualist Society, Sunday evening, at the Knights of Malta Hall. Skeptics, investigators and all interested are invited to be present. The seats are free."

In 1910, Edgar was listed as a clairvoyant with a rural practice. He was still living with Julius and Julia in Manchester. *The Boston Globe*, 30 March 1901, quoted him at the Boston Ladies' Aid Day celebration of modern Spiritualism: "My Spiritualism is not a belief, but a positive knowledge, and I desire to grow in this knowledge."

Edgar died in 1919 at the age of 63 in Manchester, New Hampshire. *The Fitchburg Sentinel* (Massachusetts), 21 January 1919, wrote, "Dr. Edgar W Emerson died at his home in Manchester, N. H. on Jan. 18 after a lingering sickness. He was well known in this city as a long time and faithful worker in the cause of Spiritualism which was his life work."

JOHN REYNOLDS FRANCIS

John Reynolds Francis was born to John and Nancy Francis of New Hope, Cayuga County, New York in 1832. His father was a blacksmith and his mother died when he was only six years old. By the age of 17, he was teaching at a school near his home. Later he tutored the family of a plantation owner in Virginia and then taught in Kansas for a short time. When he was fired from a school for his religious beliefs as a Universalist, he took a position in a printing office. By the end of the year, he oversaw the entire newspaper.

As a newspaper editor, he moved to Kansas where he worked for the *Olathe Mirror*. Because of its anti-slavery policy, ruffians from Missouri went after him and the newspaper. Francis was captured and almost killed by Captain Quantrill's Raiders before escaping. They destroyed the *Mirror* office and Francis quickly joined a cavalry company, working for General McKean. After the Civil War, he was elected chief clerk of the House of Representatives in the first Kansas Legislature and spent two years as secretary of the Senate.

In 1869, he moved to Chicago to become an editorial writer and then associate editor for the *Religio-Philosophical Journal*. He was eventually fired by Col. Bundy, the editor, because he "always abused the Bible and superlatives." He married Louisa C. Marriott in 1887 and founded his own paper, *The Progressive Thinker*, in 1889.

The Progressive Thinker was the pre-eminent Spiritualist journal from the mid-1890s on, acting for a time as the unofficial publication of the National Spiritualists Association. The journal not only covered traditional reform beliefs with Spiritualism, it exposed fraudulent mediums and took regular contributions on New Thought and occultism.

Francis was a collector of books, with "books in every room and in every available place." He was interested in both the material and spiritual worlds. He also followed closely all the scientific discoveries of the time, including radium, electricity, and wireless telegraphy. His best-known works were *A Search After God,* and a three-volume set of *The Encyclopedia of Death and Life in the Spirit World.*

Mrs. Francis, who was also on the staff of *The Progressive Thinker,* wrote in his memorial in 1910, "For more than a quarter century it was my privilege to give him such humble assistance as I might in this life-work. Together we discussed the many plans that came to his fertile brain, together we wrought for the success of those plans. Now that he has entered upon a wider field of effort, I am grateful that I for so many years was able to lighten his burden; and it is with feelings of heartfelt thankfulness that I am able to record the many kindly tributes of those who loved and labored with him."

HONORABLE ATELSTON GASTON

Atelston Gaston was born in 1838 in Castile, New York, the second of six children born to Edmon and Phylinda Gaston. He moved with his parents to Crawford County, Pennsylvania in 1854 where he attended public schools.

Athelston worked as a farmer until 1873, when he moved to Meadville, Pennsylvania and became a lumber manufacturer. He was also active in politics. He served two terms as mayor of Meadville, Pennsylvania (1891-1895) and was elected as a Democrat to the Fifty-Sixth Congress (March 4, 1899-March 3, 1901). After an unsuccessful run for reelection in 1900 to the Fifty-Seventh Congress, he returned to the lumber business.

He married Thankful Caroline Hammond and they had two daughters, Ada and Alma (who died in infancy). Both Athelston and Thankful were active Spiritualists. He served for 18 years on the Board of Directors of Lily Dale and was President of the Lily Dale Assembly for 15 years. Today, his picture hangs in honor in the Assembly Hall of Lily Dale. They had Spiritualist weddings in their home in Meadville, and in 1903 Cora L. V. Richmond and her husband were their guests. She spoke and held a private mediumship circle for a small group of friends at their home.

The Evening Republican, 15 September 1888, printed a story about Athelston and Mr. Crumrine, a local Presbyterian minister from Cochranton, bringing slates to Lily Dale to test mediums. The slates were screwed together, and the screws covered with wax. Mr. Mansfield volunteered to conduct the slate writing experiment, but they had to reschedule.

"Mr. Crumrine left the slates in charge of Mr. A. Ganton, of Meadville, Pa, who promised to hold a séance with Mansfield and report the results. Suffice it to say that Mr. Gaston held three seances with Mansfield, the medium saying that this would be necessary in order to "magnetise" the slates. At the third séance, which was held on Sunday afternoon, September 2, the medium declared that his familiar spirit told him if he would take the slate to the auditorium, where the lecture was then progressing, and form a circle, an attempt would be made to write upon the slates. Accordingly, Mr. Gaston took the slates to the auditorium, and at the close of the lecture a circle was formed on the stage and connection established by clasped hands with the audience."

Mr. Gaston took the slates home to Rev. Crumrine where they made sure the seals were intact and opened them to find a message. Part of the message to Crumrine said, "If he will investigate in the right way, he will soon find that his friends can write to him, and that this is not nor never was the devil." It was signed by Thomas Vreeland.

In October 1903, Thankful died at the age of 67 after dealing with a chronic illness for 30 years. She had been aa active Spiritualist for 45 years. Athelston was accidently killed in a hunting accident while on a trip along Lake Edward in northern Quebec, Canada, September 23, 1907. His services were conducted by Mrs. Cora L. V. Richmond of Chicago and Lyman C. Howe of Fredonia, New York.

MARGARET GAULE REIDINGER (MAGGIE GAULE)

Maggie Gaule was born about 1857 in Baltimore, Maryland to Stephen and Catherine Gaule. Her mother was widowed very early. Maggie was reared in the Catholic faith and educated in a convent. After graduating from school, she took a position as a saleswoman in a shoe store. *The Evening Sun* (Baltimore), 13 June 1910, interviewed Spiritualist, Dr. John D. Roberts. He told the paper that while Maggie was working, a man came in to buy shoes for his wife. She wrapped them up and as she handed the shoes to him, she spontaneously said, "You're going to kill the woman for whom you bought these shoes." Three days later, he shot his wife.

Afterward, Maggie met Mr. Washington A. Dansking, a prominent medium at the time. Under his guidance, her abilities improved, and she made a business of going to houses and sitting in on family seances. Raps on the tables answered questions addressed to her in sealed envelopes. Washie, a Native American, was her spirit guide. Dr. Roberts said, "…she always used her powers to help humanity. No person who was too poor to pay was ever turned away from her door when they came seeking knowledge of their dead. She made money, but she spent it for the relief of others as fast as she made it." She traveled across the eastern part of the United States, working as a test medium in different cities and Spiritualist camps.

In 1904, Maggie married August T. Reidinger in New York but was always known as Maggie Gaule to Spiritualists. Dr. Roberts said, "They will tell you that Maggie Gaule was clairaudient, which means simply that she heard clearly the voices of spirits; that she was a 'mental medium,' as distinguished from a physical medium." She was pastor of the First Spiritualist Society and later pastor of the First Ethical Society.

In *Glimpses of the Next State* (1911), author, Vice-Admiral W. Usborne Moore said, "In a quarter of an hour, Maggie Gaule came in, and, standing by the table, gave an address on the objects of spiritualism and the various faculties of mediums. She denied the power she exercised was that of telepathy. Her friends in that room brought their spirits with them, and it was from these spirits that she obtained the information which she imparted; and more to the same effect." Noted Spiritualist, Moses Hull, said she, "...has few peers and no superiors as a test medium...."

Dr. Roberts wrote, "There was no 'flying dutchman' spiritualism about her.... Windows did not open and shut in unaccountable ways. She did not sit in darkness clothed in the gown of a priestess of sombre things. She sat usually in a room filled with light—daylight as frequently as not, and told the person who had consulted her first things about the living then things about the dead." Many of her messages were given to settle family disputes and advise about business affairs and marriage, as well as find lost or stolen articles. "She seldom went into trances during the last of the thirty years in which she practiced her arts in Baltimore. The trance seances were most frequent when she was giving public seances in a hall on Saratoga street, near Pine."

Although she was a noteworthy medium, Maggie had a short life. She died in June of 1910 in New York at the age of 48.

WILLIAM W. HICKS

According to *The Light of Truth*, 1 October 1898, William W. Hicks was from Toronto, Ontario where he had a large and influential church. "Dr. Hicks is best known to Spiritualists through his addresses, notably those delivered to the throngs at Lily Dale during the past four or five years. He came into Spiritualism with a mind ripe and ready for the basic propositions of its philosophy. He had traveled in the far east and knew Orientalism as well as he knew the people. He knew the religion of the Christ. He had met many races, many people, was a scholar, linguist, teacher and student. And he came into the mighty work and brought his wealth with him and surely wherever his voice has been heard and his presence felt there has come into the lives of the people a rich and rare tonic. Such men live on the peaks. Oftentimes misunderstood some times maligned, but they never swerve."

William was also the author of several publications. *The Sanctuary* Vol. 1 and 2, was published in Boston in 1910. It was mentioned in the *Boston Evening Transcript,* 10 December 1910 as "A collection of ten essays upon the highest spiritual life. Wrote of the beatitudes of the Buddha, Sakya-Muni and Christ." About self-communion he wrote, "Do not distrust yourself, but trust, confide. Let your soul out of prison betimes. Take walks and flights into the real, into the infinite. Take walks into Nature with God. Do not wait for the decay and death of your mortal body before enjoying the freedom of the whole universe, which is your very own."

He also wrote *The Jungle-Wallah, The Thorn of Sorrow, A Valentine for the Lonely*, and *The Banner with the New Device*, about women and their place in the world. The Boston Globe, 14 April 1913 wrote, "Persons interested in New Thought, psychometry, psychotherapy and the modern rise of woman will find much of interest in William W. Hicks' new book...."

The records of William's birth, family, or death could not be found, but his impact on Spiritualism during his lifetime was profound.

Benjamin B. Hill

Benjamin B. Hill was born to Benjamin and Rebecca Hill in 1830 in Middlesex, Massachusetts. His first marriage was to Sarah A. Steele in 1850. They had five children while Benjamin worked as a machinist in Chicopee, Massachusetts. He was successful in his trade, and holder of roughly 75 patents related to the stamp trade. By 1867, he was a manufacturer of Seal Presses in Springfield, Massachusetts and his travels took him as far west as California. He formed the B. B. Hill Manufacturing Company in 1880, which employed 18 skilled workers.

Benjamin's life was not without tragedy. In 1875, his youngest daughter, Sarah, died at the age of 15. He and his wife divorced soon afterward. By 1880, he had married his second wife, Nellie E. Channing who had also been married before to a man named Stafford. The Hills moved to Philadelphia about 1882 when Benjamin relocated his business there. They had the means to travel to Europe at least twice.

Benjamin's interest in Spiritualism began before the death of his daughter. He was a delegate to the National Spiritualists Convention as early as 1873 and a well-respected early pioneer of the Spiritualist movement in the United States. He was also active in the Camp Meeting Association in Maine. An 1881 newspaper account stated that "Dr. Abbie E Cutter on her travels spent a few weeks at the home of B. B. Hill and his wife in Springfield, Mass. Mrs. Hill who was formerly a public medium, is doing a great deal for the cause of Spiritualism. A great interest has been awakened in Springfield by the book of Samuel Bowles."

At some point, Benjamin and Nellie adopted Mercy C. Cadwallader as their daughter. In the 1890s, Cadwallader lived in Philadelphia where she worked for the Oriental Publishing Company. She was involved with the publishing of *Antiquity Unveiled* by J. M. Roberts. It was here that Cadwallader became interested in Spiritualism. Cadwallader joined the National Spiritualist Association (NSA) which was organized in 1893, and in 1894 she was elected honorary Vice-President.

Unfortunately, Nellie died in 1898 of "fatty degeneration of the heart" and Benjamin remained a widower the remainder of his life.

He sponsored the publication of the book by Boston Banner of Light Publishing Co., *The Christ Question Settled or Jesus, Man Medium, Martyr,* written by J. M. Peebles in 1899. Benjamin said of Peebles book, "Now we come to those historical characters to which Dr. Peebles in his book refers to as witnesses to prove the authenticity of the historical Jesus. He and others point to the mutilated histories of these celebrated characters for proof, but they now speak to us off-hand from spirit life. This I consider direct testimony; therefore, it should take precedence of all book testimony that has been manipulated by priestcraft."

Benjamin died in 1913 at the age of 83 while living in Chicago with Mercy C. Cadwallader and her husband. Services were held at the Temple of the First Association of Spiritualists of Philadelphia on 12 July 1913. In his will, he stipulated that he would be buried at Northwood Cemetery, in a plot that he bequeathed to Cadwallader.

LYMAN C. HOWE

Lyman C. Howe was born in Butternuts, New York in 1832 to Jared and Clarissa Howe. They couldn't afford a good education for all of their ten children but raised them as strict Calvinists who lived by the Bible. When Lyman was ten, his mother died, and the family separated. Lyman went to live with Perry Aylsworth for nearly three years before moving in with his brother who lived in Hornell, New York. He attended public school and in 1851 began teaching school until his health failed him.

Beginning in 1853, Lyman trained as a Spiritualist medium and began work as an inspirational speaker. His first open public lecture was in the Free Church at Lama near Fredonia, New York. Because of his shyness, during the first few years of his work most of his lectures were in rhyme. He did not expect to be successful, traveled 5-20 miles on foot to give private readings, and frequently wasn't paid. But by the end of 1858, he had regular speaking engagements in several New York towns.

In 1862, he married Sarah E. North and they had a daughter, Sarah Maude born in 1867. A year later, they moved to Fredonia. By then Lyman's inspirational speaking was taking him around the country. He spoke in at least 17 states and cities, including Titusville, Pennsylvania; Chicago; Kansas City; several cities in New York state including New York City; and Washington, DC, spending about a year in each. He wrote for many periodicals, including *The Sunbeam, Banner of Light* and *Psychic Review*. He also held public debates with Rev. William Rogers of Gowanda, New York, Rev. Niles of Corry, Pennsylvania and Uriah Clark of Nunda Station, New York.

In Light of Truth, vol. 20, no. 5, 1897, Lyman wrote: "I first realized phenomenal mediumship in 1854. My sight had become subject to unseen influences and would answer questions, oral or mental, while no other part of my body or mind seemed to be afflicted at all. Then followed a series of phases, automatic writing, personating, talking. Immediately after I began to talk it developed rhyme of a very perfect rhythm and meter, some of it arose to the standard of poetry. Then prophesy, and often giving names, dates and personal communications, called tests. Answering mental questions was a very common and successful phase."

Lyman was one of the first speakers at Alden's Grove and served for twenty-five years at Lily Dale without missing a season. In *Cassadaga its History and Teaching*, A.W. McCoy wrote, "His services have been required in all of the largest cities as well as in the smaller towns and villages, at all of which he has drawn large and intelligent audiences. His inspiration is of the highest and purest order." Lyman died in 1910 at the age of seventy-five after many years of dedicated service.

Moses Hull and Mattie Brown Sawyer

Moses Hull was born in 1835 in Waldo, Ohio, the seventh child of Dr. James and Mary Hull. The Hulls moved to Missouri when he was a toddler and then Indiana where he had only rudimentary schooling. The family was Baptist on both sides, but when Moses was in his teens, his father became a member of the United Brethren Church. He opened his house to visitors and church gatherings.

Moses traveled between Ohio and Indiana and eventually became interested in the Seventh-day Adventist religion. He collected a group of believers near Wabash, among them being Cynthia Ann Conde. Within a few months, they were married but she died of sickness in 1854. His traveling continued to the southern part of the state where he next met Elvira Lightner. They married in 1855 and had four daughters over the next decade.

Moses officially joined the Seventh-day Adventist Church in 1857 and became a prominent minister and debater for the denomination. He traveled extensively and was sent to assist C.W. Sperry in New York who had been sickened by hemorrhages in his lungs. During that time, he met many Spiritualists and began to doubt his beliefs. The Adventists insisted any spiritual phenomena was the work of the devil. Moses decided otherwise.

By 1865, Moses withdrew his membership from the Adventist church and began to use the Bible to support the Spiritualist cause. He argued that if Spiritualism was the work of the devil, so was the Bible. According to the *Vermont Journal* (Windsor), January 1874, Dr. Uriah Clark and Moses Hull had a debate on the merits of "so-called Spiritualism" in the town hall. "Mr. H. was much superior to his opponent."

His new interest in Spiritualism led to many published books, and he worked with several periodicals, including *The Progressive Age*, *The Religio-Philosophical Journal*, and *Spiritual Rostrum*. His books included *The Encyclopedia of Biblical Spiritualism*, and *Our Bible, Who Wrote It, When, How and Where?* It was during this time that Elvira and Moses agreed that their philosophies of life did not coincide. Elvira obtained a legal divorce and remarried a few years later.

Moses met Mattie Sawyer while they were busy running public meetings. Martha (Mattie) Brown was born New Hampshire in 1840 to Henry E. Browne. She married C.C.B. Sawyer, a carpenter, in 1858 in Templeton, Massachusetts, but was single by the time she met Moses. Following a scandal about his divorce, they married in 1872.

Three years later, the scandal still followed them. In a 21 January 1875 clipping in *The Manchester Journal*, Brick Pomeroy rails against Spiritualism for destroying families. "Spiritualism leads to free Love, adultery and infidelity." He said it "has no churches, no colleges other than houses of prostitution, where its Hull and Woodhulls can study the ministry. It has no direct line of policy, but is broken, twisted, fragmentary, and at war against itself in all its teachings." He continued: "One of its recognized captains is Moses Hull, who left a decent family after he became a Spiritualist, to practice and to preach adultery as a religion."

The Lake Massebesic Camp Meeting was just one of the projects Moses and Mattie ran while traveling the country as missionaries. They lived in Boston, Buffalo, and Whitewater, Wisconsin. They helped found the Morris Pratt Institute, and Moses was its president in 1902. Moses also became a national leader of the Greenback Labor Party which attempted to secure rights for farmers, workers and women. He ran for Congress in 1906 on the ticket of the Socialist Party but was unsuccessful.

While living in San Jose, Moses died in January of 1907. In March of the same year, Mattie presented a talk entitled "Do Spirits Return?" at the People's Psychic Conference in Burbank Hall, and "Is Spiritualism all Sufficient? to The Spiritual Society of Truthseekers in Los Angeles. She married J. A. Marvin about 1911 and died 10 years later, in February 1921 at the age of 82. She was known throughout the U.S. and Canada as a spiritualist and one of the founders of the Morris Pratt School of Spiritualism in Whitewater, Wisconsin.

JENNIE HAGAN JACKSON

An article in *The Light of Truth,* vol. 13, no. 4, 1893, wrote that Jennie Bennitt Hagan Jackson was born in Lowell, Massachusetts in 1860. Her father passed away when she was only ten months old. Mrs. Janet Hagans's sister, Jane Hoyt, came to live with them and the women purchased a small cottage in South Royalton, Vermont.

During the winter of 1863-64, Jennie began showing signs of mediumistic ability. All her relatives were Spiritualists, including her mother and aunt who were mediums. Jennie said that "she felt when spirit hands touched and caressed her, what she heard when they laughed in her company, and many other things of interest. At four years of age, she saw and heard much, but was so weak and frail they dared not urge her development on either spirit or mortal side."

Once in school, she began to see spirits, including Dr. Hoyt, her father, and Mr. Jasper Arren, an Englishman. Hoyt promised that Jennie would "never want for the comforts of life" but her health remained poor. Her mother and aunt sat in a silent circle on Thursday nights, hoping to heal her and aid in her development. When she was 11, she had a hemorrhage in her lungs and her family feared the worst would happen. The spirits were protecting her, and she recovered before they moved to Nebraska in 1873. There she regained her health and attended school.

Jennie gave her first public lecture when she was 13 in Arlington, Nebraska. She continued to lecture while in trance and gave impromptu poems on subjects given to her by the audience. In 1875, she travelled to Wisconsin and Ohio where she had relatives. She lectured almost every night. In 1876, she returned to Vermont with her mother. She attended school while going to adjoining towns to lecture. She was also involved in the temperance movement.

In 1887, she joined the Lake Pleasant Camp meeting for the first time. Other camp meetings followed, and she travelled as far west as Missouri and Iowa, and even went to Canada. In 1891, at the Lily Dale camp meeting, she was married to Bradford D. Jackson of Grand Rapids, Michigan.

Jackson was born in Sullivan, Ohio and was a landscape and scenic view photographer who began his career taking portraits in Grand Rapids, Michigan. "A vast audience took part in the ceremony, and all joined in good will, love, and harmony toward the newly wedded pair." They lived in Grand Rapids with Jennie's mother. "Mrs. Jennie B. Hagan Jackson is continuing her work, and her husband is a great aid to her, whose profession is that of an artist and photographer. There new line is in connection with a stereopticon and finely illustrated lectures from photographic views which Mr. Jackson makes."

They were putting together a book of views of various Spiritualist camp meetings. An album still exists that contains photos taken at four camps: Onset Bay Grove, Lake Pleasant, Nickerson's Grove and Queen City Park.

By 1898, Jennie was a Spiritualist leader in Fort Worth, Texas, and building a spiritual center. The attendance was large and prospering. Bradford filed for divorce in 1899, citing "cruelty and desertion" as the cause. Jennie quickly married Horace Daniel Brown, a traveling salesman, the following year. They maintained an inn. The same year, Jennie attended the International Jubilee at the Golden Jubilee Celebration of Spiritualism in Rochester, New York. Jennie and Cora L. V. Richmond gave impromptu poems from a subject given by the audience, including "The Sinking and Rising of the Maine", and for an encore "Mountain and Valley."

Jennie died in 1907 in El Campo, Texas while still in charge of a parish. The *Herald and News* (Randolf, Vermont), February 7, 1907, wrote, "At an early age Mrs. Brown developed a marvelous intuitive faculty of mind, empowering her to deliver a strong and well composed poem, upon any subject given her without premeditation or hesitation and always very gracefully. In later years she commenced to lecture and preach and had become noted as an interesting speaker." Jennie got blood poisoning from an injured knee and died a few days after the injury, leaving a "fine estate and beautiful home." Horace Brown died a decade later.

ABBY A. JUDSON

Abby A. Judson was born in 1835 in Myanmar (Burma) to Rev. Dr. Adoniram and Sarah Hall Judson, both Baptist missionaries at the time. In 1841, one of her younger brothers, Henry, passed while they were on a trip to India. That was followed by the death of her mother in 1845 while they were in the harbor of St. Helena Island. Her father remarried and the family returned to Burma, where her father died in 1850.

Abby was educated at several private schools along the east coast of the United States. She worked as a governess and then teacher in New England from 1853-1879. After a year traveling in Europe, she founded the Judson Female Institute in Minneapolis in 1879. She became a Spiritualist in 1887, closed her seminary, and began giving private lessons and devoting herself to Spiritualism.

In 1890, after attending a camp meeting in Clinton, Iowa, she was inspired to create a new Spiritualist association in Minneapolis. Since she wasn't a medium or healer, the group decided she would be the one to educate the public with informational writings and lectures. She described her process of writing in *Why She Became a Spiritualist: Twelve Lectures*. "On these two afternoons, when ready to write, she deadened her door-bell, darkened her study with close curtains, 'entered her closet and shut to' the curtain, and there played on her organ in the dark, until she saw waves of magnetic light, resembling the aurora borealis shimmering over the Arctic sky. Shen then went to her desk, raised the curtain just enough for her to see to write, and then wrote notes, words and sometimes whole sentences, without conscious effort."

By 1891, Abby was speaking in public. A dozen of her lectures and her biography were published in the book, *Why She Became a Spiritualist: Twelve Lectures* (1895). Other books included: *The Bridge Between Two Worlds*

(1894), *Development of Mediumship by Terrestrial Magnetism,* and *From Night to Morn; or an Appeal to the Baptist Church.* Her lectures included topics such as: "What is Spiritualism," "Do Spiritualists Believe in God," "Personal Evidences of Spiritualism," "Unreasonable Dogmas," and "What is Death."

Abby compared Spiritualism to other religions in *Why She Became a Spiritualist: Twelve Lectures,* saying: "All these religions have their limitations. These limitations arise from narrowness of doctrine; from a servile deference to one man, its founder; or from race restrictions. Spiritualism, on the other hand, is utterly comprehensive. It is a cult, or rather a knowledge, that reaches all men in all conditions, in all countries, and in all ages of the world. Yes, it goes beyond this physical world, and embraces in its divine sway, all spirits out of the body, and all spirits in all the universe."

Abby died a tragic death when a lamp accidently overturned next to her bed while she was reading. Some of the burning oil fell on the bed and ignited her clothes. She ran from the house, but died from her burns in December of 1902 in Arlington, New Jersey.

DAVID MILES KING

David King was born in Bennington, Vermont to John and Alcesta King in 1833. He moved to Ohio in the early 1850s and married Lucy Everett in 1855. David bought a farm in Hiram Township, two miles east of Mantua Station, and became active in the local Grange (Patrons of Husbandry) which dealt with the concerns of farmers. He was also active in the Temperance Society and Spiritualism.

During the mid to late 1870s, David lectured on prohibition and spiritual progression. He held a meeting in 1877 at his home asking if there is life beyond death. According to the *Democratic Press* (Ravenna, OH), 19 April 1877, "on six successive evenings, by the visible and tangible appearance of a score or more of those who long since experienced the change common to mortals, and called death. Being materialized in form and feature, they were able to give the most convincing tests of their power to manifest themselves, and prove that they still live and take an interest in the welfare of their friends in this life." Over two hundred people attended the meetings to witness the phenomena.

The *Summit County Beacon,* 12 Jan 1887, reported that at the Summit County Pomona Grange "scientific lecturer, D.M. King of Mantua Station, Portage County, who hopefully believes that the two million Grange workers, with their increasing numbers, will be able to counteract the tendencies of both anarchists and monopolists to disrupt this government." He also discussed selling and shipping farm products from the station.

During the 1880s, David studied phrenology and gave lectures across Ohio on the subject. He joined with Milton C. Danforth and toured Ohio and Michigan. Milton C. Danforth was born in Hudson Township,

Summit County, Ohio. He was also involved with the Grange and later became involved with the Spiritualist movement.

Telegraph-Forum (Bucyrus, Ohio), 18 Mar 1887, reported that "Prof. D. M. King left Thursday for Marengo, where he will do missionary work in the cause of Spiritualism. During his lecture here he delivered three lectures on Spiritualism and kindred subjects which evinced great thought and learning, while his practical demonstration of his theories were startling and convincing. His psychometrical readings are the most wonderful ever given in this country. He made many friends in this place who would like to see and hear more of his mysterious profession." In 1889, he taught a Phrenological Science course at Cleveland Business College.

David was said to have organized seven different spiritualist camps and that his most successful work had been at Maple Dell Park in Ohio. He is also the founder of the Cleveland Anthropological Institute, an incorporated school for special work with no connection with any religious body. *Akron Beacon Journal*, 6 August 1896, said that he continued his lectures until 1902 and died in 1910 after being accidentally hit by a train engine on November 13th.

ELIZABETH SANFORD KINNE

Elizabeth B. Price was born in 1828 in Vermont, one of the seven children of John and Asenath Price. When she was a child, the family moved their home to Three Rivers, St. Joseph County, Michigan. Elizabeth married Lewis Sanford about 1845, and they had a daughter and two sons before Lewis died in Sumner, Tennessee during the Civil War in 1863. Elizabeth eventually married physician Andrew Kinne in 1877 in Cook County, Illinois. By 1880, they were living in Colon, Michigan with her son, L. W. Sanford, from her first marriage. Elizabeth was listed in the census as a physician at that time.

Elizabeth was listed in the directory of Deceased American Physicians (1804-1929) as an Allopath and other sources refer to her as a magnetic healer. Magnetic healing was a popular curative at the time. Both she and Andrew were active in the Spiritualist community, attending camp meetings at Lake Park and South Haven in the 1890s. In 1893, Andrew conducted a séance test, and the couple traveled from Illinois to Missouri to visit her children.

Andrew died in 1895 at 72 years old, but Elizabeth continued her work as a doctor and magnetic healer from her home in Dwight, Illinois. On February 21, 1913, *The Kansas City Times* published Elizabeth's obituary. It stated that, "Mrs. Elizabeth B. Kinne, 86 years old, the mother of E.J. Sanford, former president of the Union Depot Company, died of heart failure at her home in Excelsior Springs last night. Mrs. Kinne was a pioneer physician in Illinois, having started a practice in Dwight more than sixty years ago. She moved to Excelsior Springs ten years ago." She was buried at Mt. Washington cemetery.

BENJAMIN F. LEE

Captain Benjamin F. Lee was born 1835 in the state of New York and enlisted to fight with the Union in the Civil War in August of 1862, in Geneva, New York. He was in the 126th Infantry. Benjamin was wounded and imprisoned at Harpers Ferry in September 1862, and discharged in 1864. He moved to Sandusky about 6 years after the war where he practiced law with Judge Cooper K. Watson. He was elected prosecuting attorney in 1873 and served one term.

Benjamin invested in the Arizona Gold Mining Company and lost his entire investment. By 1880, according to the Sandusky, Ohio census, he was a 45-year-old lawyer living at a hotel run by H. W. Powers. By that time, Benjamin was interested in the Spiritualist movement. He became involved with the development of the Lake Brady Spiritualist camp in Mantua, Ohio and was listed as a Mantua attorney in 1892.

In 1896, Benjamin was President of the Brady Lake Spiritual Association. "This association has in view the establishment of a camp or resort, where thought may be fully expressed and as freely criticized; where the lowest may look for aid and aspire to become the highest; where goodness, purity, wisdom and all the attributes of the truthful soul may be taught and practiced; and where spiritualism in its most comprehensive application shall be fostered."

Unfortunately, tragedy befell him. The *Akron Beacon Journal*, 22 Apr 1898, wrote: "The cottage of Captain Benjamin F. Lee, president of the Lake Brady Spiritualists' Association was burned to the ground Thursday Evening and this morning the charred remains of the captain were found in the ruins.

"The cottage was the finest at the lake and was occupied by Captain Lee the year round. It was finely furnished and contained a valuable library of several hundred volumes. A number of boys discovered the fire at 7:30 o'clock last evening. When they arrived at the cottage they found the rear part in flames. Breaking in the front door they called for Lee but failed to receive an answer. They were driven out by the flames and the cottage was soon entirely consumed without any of its contents being saved. The loss will be close to $1,500."

Coroner said Benjamin probably fainted because of preexisting heart problems and knocked over lamp. At the time of his death, he was well-known among Spiritualists throughout the country, especially in Akron. He had lived in both Cleveland and Mantua.

CHALMERS P. AND MARY T. LONGLEY

Chalmers P. Longley was born about 1827 in Hawley, Massachusetts, son of Joshua and Elizabeth (his second wife) Longley. Mary T. Shelhamer was born in 1853 to John D. and Mary A. Shelhamer in Boston, Massachusetts. Mary married the much older Chalmers in 1888 when he was known as a music composer.

Mary was already working as a medium when she married Chalmers. Her mediumship was never questioned. Father Pierpont, her spirit guide, as well as her more ancient guides, affirmed that Jesus did exist, and that they had seen him in the spiritual world. Mary was active in the Boston Spiritualist community. She was a guest at Lake Pleasant multiple times, attended the 47th anniversary celebration at the Boston Spiritualist Temple, and addressed the National Spiritualists Association third annual convention in 1895. She also authored *Outside the Gates, Nameless, When the Morning Comes,* and *Only a Step.*

In 1890, Mary wrote to the *Temple Messenger*, vol 1 no 2, October 1890, "The lyceum movement is one that by this time should have taken hold of the popular mind—at least among Spiritualists and Liberalists—and have made its power felt to an enlarged degree. No doubt the entertainment which the Children's Progressive Lyceum has afforded to its attendants during the last quarter of a century has in many instances been appreciated, but, as a whole, the question remains; Has the lyceum movement proven to be all that its projectors hoped for in its earlier years?" She argued that the lyceum must be both instructive and entertaining and hoped that the *Temple Messenger* would provide some of the information needed.

While Mary was involved with her mediumship, Chalmers continued with his musical career. They moved to California. In 1894, he published

Echoes of the World of Song, "fifty-eight choice compositions with music and chorus suitable for our spiritual lyceums, etc." It was sold by Colby and Rich of Los Angeles. An 1896 advertisement in the *Banner of Light* announced that C. Payton Longly, well known composer, published "A Fine Musical Tribute of three compositions. The beautiful song dedicated to the memory of the veteran editor, Luther Colby, is a companion piece to that standard melody 'Only a Thin Veil Between Us.; That inscribed to Mrs. Clara H Banks bears the title 'Only a Curtain Between,' and that to Arthur Hodges, 'Oh! What Will it Be to Be There?'"

The *Banner of Light,* vol 81, no 14, 1897 wrote, "Mrs. M. T. Longley, the well-known medium, formerly of the *Banner of Light*, is located in Los Angeles, Cal., as will be seen by her advertisement on our fifth page, and frequently lectures for the First Spiritual Society there. Mrs. Longley's work as psychometrist, healer and business medium is well known. Her readings for spiritual advice, the cure of obsession and the development of mediumship are given by the influence of spirit John Pierpont, those for business and personal matters by Lotela, Hareball and others of her efficient band, while she diagnoses and prescribes for disease under the influence of her medical guide, old Dr. John Warren, who has attended her for twenty years."

By 1900, Mary and Chalmers had moved back east and were living in Washington, D.C. She was a secretary for the National Spiritualist Association. In 1920, Mary and Chalmers were boarders with the Fugitt family. Chalmers died that January at the age of 93. Mary continued to work. In 1920, at the national convention in Chicago she gave a lecture entitled, "The Theory of Psychic Glands." In 1924 she gave lectures in Montana and California. Mary's last adventure was a voyage to France in 1926. She passed away in 1928 at the age of 75.

AMELIA H. COLBY LUTHER

Amelia Hunt was born in 1829 in New York to Zachariah and Amelia Hunt of Erie County. She married farmer Hylon Colby in 1849 and they had 4 children. By 1860, the family had moved to Lake County, Indiana where Hylon continued farming. Amelia became involved with the Spiritualist movement. In 1867, Mr. J. H. Luther wrote that Amelia was "a good woman and an earnest efficient worker in the field of Progress." She was listed as a trance speaker appearing in Penville, Indiana in 1869.

In 1870, Amelia listed her profession as a lecturer in the census. Three of her teenaged children were at home working on the farm. Apparently, the marriage did not last. Hylon remarried in 1875, and Amelia continued with her lectures. During June and July of 1878 in Winchester, Indiana a publication announced: "She will answer calls to lecture or hold grove meetings anywhere in the state. She is accompanied by Mrs. O. Smith, who is reputed to be a fine singer and guitarist."

Amelia married James H. Luther in Indiana in 1887. She was more than just a Spiritualist minister and trance lecturer, she was an abolitionist, suffragist, free thinker, and traveled throughout the country giving lectures in both trance and normal states. She named the Cassadaga Lake Free Association which later became Lily Dale, and she was one of the founders of Camp Chesterfield. According to the *Anderson Daily Bulletin*, 20 May 1954, there was a gathering of over 50 Spiritualists in 1885 who met in Anderson, Indiana. They organized the Indiana Association of Spiritualists or Chesterfield Spiritualist Camp. Amelia and her husband James were members.

During the 1880-90s, Amelia lectured at many locations including at Crown Point, Indiana; the Ladies' Industrial Society of the Boston Spiritual Temple; and in 1895 at Berkeley Hall where she gave a lecture entitled "If the is no God, what force in the universe creates matter?" In 1885, she spoke at Neshaminy Falls Spiritualist Camp; the topic was "Crime: Its cause and remedy."

Amelia was described in the *Banner of Light,* vol. 63 no. 7, 28 April 1888, as a "tall, well-kept, white-haired lady of apparently about fifty years, in a clear tone and with much fervor and animation held the audience, without manuscript, for over an hour." Her article in the publication spoke about Rev. Mills, the religious hierarchy that ministers support, and his uninformed opinion about female Spiritualists. "As the church teaches, the less we know the more we believe, and the more we believe the less we know." She continued, "Spiritualism came to protect human life and reason, and that grandest of all things human, woman, the mother of nations. It is an established fact. It demands investigation. Dare anybody say it has not stood the test of the greatest scientific minds? This is not the only age when these great truths were known. Let mediums live and there will be produced some of the most remarkable phenomena ever known. The reverend gentleman knows that as Spiritualism marches on his business is gone."

Amelia H. Luther died 26 Dec 1897 in Muncie, Indiana after making a large impact on Spiritualism.

Dr. William A. Mansfield

William A. Mansfield was born in 1859 to farmers Amos and Ann Mansfield in Ravenna, Michigan. He became one of the best-known slate writing mediums in the country. According to *The Akron Beacon Journal,* July 21, 1893, He had "an extensive acquaintance in spiritual circles and is honored and respected everywhere. He is yet a young man but has been before the public for 11 years in his chosen work. He spent two years in the Bryant & Statton business college in Buffalo, after which he went to Boston, where he spent two years in the college of oratory, graduating from that celebrated institution in 1889. He is now a junior in the Huron Street Hospital College at Cleveland. Mr. Mansfield has traveled extensively and has visited nearly all the large cities in the United States." An 1890 advertisement stated: "William A. Mansfield. Medium for Independent Slate Writing, Hotel in Boston, Private sittings. Private Home Circles."

William's 1893 wedding was held at Brady's Lake Spiritualist Camp according to the *Akron Beacon Journal,* 21 July 1893. "The bright, warm sun, as it rose from the east yesterday morning, peeped through the tall and stately forest trees at Lake Brady, and cast occasional rays down on a happy, expectant throng, which was assembled to witness an interesting ceremony, one seldom celebrated at a summer resort. It was nothing more or less than a marriage ceremony, in which a well-known, popular and beloved member of the spiritual camp led to the altar a handsome, charming young girl from Michigan. The groom was Will. A. Mansfield and the bride Miss Lenno A. Moray, both of Grand Rapids, Mich." His brother John Orton Mansfield was a groomsman. About 250 people attended.

A son was born to the couple in 1894 and a daughter in 1895. William presented lectures and conducted slate writing at Lily Dale, Grand Ledge Spiritualist's Camp in Michigan, and Maple Dell Park in Mantua, Ohio in the 1890s. In 1897, at Maple Dell Park, he "gave a light séance for physical manifestation." He spent the season at the camp.

William advertised in *Light of Truth*: "Homeopathic Treatment compounded clairvoyantly for each case. Send name, age, sex, leading symptoms for Free Diagnosis and 'Methods of Cure.'" Another advertisement stated: "Dr Mansfield. Homeopathic treatment compounded clairvoyantly for each case. Send name, age, sex, leading symptoms for free diagnosis and methods of cure. Cedar avenue in Cleveland."

By 1900, William was a widower living with his daughter at his brother John's home in Cleveland. He moved to Barberton, Ohio where he was health commissioner for 25 years. By 1930, he had been suffering from an illness for two years. The 1930, *Akron Beacon Journal* reported on William's death at the age of 72 as a suicide, using exhaust fumes from his automobile.

DR. JAMES V. MANSFIELD

James V. Mansfield was born in Dudley, Massachusetts in 1817 to farmers Jera and Lucretia Mansfield. The family claimed to be related to Lord Mansfield who rid England of Slavery. James' ability as a medium started at an early age when he began seeing spirits. He suffered from a sickness during his teen years and was thought to be close to death seven times. He was an avid reader during his sickness, but never received any schooling until after he recovered at the age of twenty. He attended an academic school for about six months, studying English. After that, he became a clerk at a country store until he was 22.

James married Mary Hopkinson in 1847, and they had three children. They endured many financial struggles, and he was impelled at times to travel in search of work. He taught penmanship in Virginia and the Carolinas before returning to the store where he worked for several more years.

After moving to Boston, James became a prominent member of the Spiritualist movement. He was listed in the fourth Annual Spiritualist Register in 1860 as a medium who provided spirit communications through letter writing and earned the title, "spirit postmaster." Those who wished to communicate with the departed could have a séance with him in person or mail a letter to the spirit in care of Mansfield. In the latter case, he would provide answers to unopened letters. He granted sittings if they didn't interfere with his regular work. After some time, he became so popular that he decided to make mediumship his business.

James left Boston to travel, visiting the major cities in the eastern United States. Then he went to the Pacific coast and remained there for three years. While he traveled, he wrote home to his wife. His letters to her totaled over 16,000 pages. From 1866-1869, he also responded to

31,000 letters, 21,000 which were hand written and sent free, without any payment or any demand for payment. According to the *Banner of Light*, "As the answers he sent are written very coarsely on printing paper, postage stamps form no inconsiderable item in these expenses, sometimes as high as twenty cents being put upon one letter...."

Mansfield was both admired and disdained for his "talents." He also referred to himself as a "test medium," providing free communications for skeptics. In 1885, he was studied by the University of Pennsylvania's Seybert Commission, which was established to investigate spiritualist phenomena. After observing him, Dr. Horace Howard Furness of the Commission concluded in the official report that he was at best a charlatan.

Others stood by him. In the *Banner of Light*, 7 November 1885, vol. 58 no. 8, it stated, "Of the many whom we have personally known to have tested his mediumship, we can refer to a no less experienced and accurate an observer then Rev. John Pierpont, who frequently, during his earth-life, held private seances with Mr. Mansfield and received such undoubted evidence of his mediumship as to go far toward firmly convincing him of the truth of Spiritualism."

James Mansfield died in 1899 in Ipswich, Massachusetts at the age of 82. He wrote to Mr. Jay Chaapel, "I have been trying to live for the last half century to make the world better from my having lived in it, but if so it remains to be seen....Forty-six years have I labored for Spiritualism, and have never rusted. I have written 700,000 communications in 15 different languages on paper five inches wide to three and a half feet in length, which, if pasted together, would have extended twice around the globe. My public labors have ended, though with few exceptions, I do write for packages from abroad occasionally. I have lost the sight of my right eye, have but partial use of my right arm, and my lower limbs have become almost useless from paralysis. I am 82 years old, have no fear of death and have been looking forward for the change the last ten years."

DR. AURELIA MARVIN

Aurelia Desiree Tolman was born in 1820 to Elijah and Florilla Tolman of Erie County, New York. Her father was one of the first settlers of the county and purchased a large tract of land there. In 1839, Aurelia married Dr. Harvey B. Marvin who had been born into a farming family in Vermont. He was one of the first doctors in America to adopt homeopathic medicine.

By 1850, they were living in Evans, Erie County, New York. They had four children: Frances, Horace, LaDor and LaRoy. The family moved to Grand Rapids, Michigan where Aurelia and her daughter, Francis, were practicing mediums. Francis developed her mediumship skills as early as 1854, but she died in 1866. Aurelia's husband, Harvey, died a four years later. By then, Horace, LaRoy and LaDor were practicing homeopathic physicians and Spiritualists. Horace lived in Sioux City, Iowa, LaRoy in Muskegon and LaDor in Grand Rapids, Michigan.

Aurelia was one of America's early women physicians, listing herself as a mental and physical healer. She continued her practice into the 1890s and was listed in the 1895 Grand Rapids Directory as Aurelia D. Marvin (widow of Harvey B. Marvin) physician, living at 264 E. Bridge Street in the city.

Aurelia Marvin died in 1903 at the age of 83. In the *Progressive Thinker*, 22 August 1903, Lyman C. Howe wrote about Mrs. Dr. Aurelia Dewey Marvin, whom he had known for forty years. He referred to her as a "remarkable psychic and healer of the sick." Her husband graduated as a regular physician before adopting homeopathic medicine. He was practicing in Buffalo when the Fox sisters became prominent. "Mrs.

Marvin became a medium, had visions, and soon developed remarkable powers for healing the sick by laying on of hands."

One spirit, Howe said, came to her and told her to change her pastor's pro-slavery thoughts. "She had a long interview with her pastor, and was so inspired that, with the help of the spirits, she penetrated the prejudices of the preacher and completely revolutionized his political creed and all his preaching on the subject of slavery was reversed."

Howe continued, "I knew a young man in Laona, who was paralyzed from his hips down, by a sunstroke, while in the army, serving his country. Physicians could not help him. As a last resort, and a forlorn hope, he went to the home of Dr. Marvin, then in Erie County, N. Y. He stayed four weeks, during which time Mrs. Marvin treated him without medicine, and he returned home perfectly cured. Many hundreds if not thousands, could testify of her powers from personal experience. I have been one that she has blessed in that way."

THEODORE J. MAYER

Theodore J. Mayer was born in Geneva, Switzerland in 1846 and received his education in public schools and colleges. After he graduated, he worked for a large bank as a correspondent and bookkeeper. He immigrated to the United States in 1866, married Susanna Hitz in 1876, and they had two sons. Susanna died soon after her second son's birth. Theodore continued to live with the Hitz family and worked at W. M. Galt and Co., overseeing the wholesale flour department. He later became a full partner in the business.

Theodore was one of the members of the committee who started the movement to create a national Spiritualism association. He was elected Treasurer of the National Spiritualists' Association (NSA) of the United States several times and was Vice President of the First Spiritual Association of Washington D.C. In 1900, while treasurer of the NSA, he offered to donate a house which functioned as the national headquarters, providing they raised the $10,000 needed "to carry on the National work." He was also instrumental in buying a sanitarium from A. P. Spinney to house the sick.

According to Theodore's obituary in the *Washington Evening Star*, 13 March 1907, "Mr. Mayer had been actively engaged in the work of upbuilding this city and increasing its prosperity since he came here in 1866. He usually took a leading part in philanthropic efforts and was especially interested in the welfare of east Washington, in which his home was located. He was nearly sixty-one years of age. It is remarked that he retained his mental and physical vigor to a remarkable degree, and until stricken by the ailment which ended in his death was an active man of affairs. He was a member of the Masonic fraternity, a director of the Eastern Dispensary and Casualty Hospital, and also a member of the directorate of the Central National Bank, the Union Trust Company and the George Washington University. For fifteen years he had been president of the Swiss Benevolent Association, and as such is said to have 'carried sunshine into many saddened homes.'"

According to the *Sunflower*, 30 March 1907, Mayer "did not forget to bless and honor Spiritualism in the distribution of his estate. As is well known, Mr. Mayer was a self-made man. He did not acquire any of the large fortune he left, by inheritance or gift, but he made it by unfailing toil of hands and brain and by his judicious investments. He was essentially a clear-cut mentality, sound financier and staunch Spiritualist." He deeded three houses to the NSA upon his death.

HONORABLE LUTHER V. AND SARAH MOULTON

Luther V. Moulton was born in 1845 in Case County Michigan to Bridgeman Moulton. He enlisted in the Union Army but had to leave because of poor health. After the war, he became a sailor on the Great Lakes, operating a schooner. He married Sarah A. Armstrong in 1865, and became a photographer in Wisconsin. They eventually moved to Grand Rapids in 1875 where he opened his own photography studio. He ran and was elected to the Michigan state legislature on the Greenback ticket in 1879. Afterward, he began the study of law and opened a practice in 1890, specializing in patent law.

The Herald Palladium (Benton Harbor, MI), 7 November 1887, stated that Luther attended a meeting of the Southeastern Michigan Association of Spiritualists and "...the audience listened attentively to an interesting lecture by Mr. Moulton on the theme 'Searching for the Infinite.' The speaker reviewed in a general way the origin of the world and traced the outgrowth in mankind of the desire for knowledge, particularly of the existence to come. He cited the universal belief in an unseen world and the faith in immortality that has progressed from the very birth of man to the present, until it now finds its highest proof and exemplification in the demonstrations and discoveries of modern spiritualism."

Along with being a regular speaker at Fraser Grove, Luther spoke at many meetings across the state. In 1887, he attended Southwestern Association of Spiritualists at Benton Harbor. Over the next decade, he lectured at Lake Park near Detroit, the Grand Rapids state meeting, progressive thinker meetings, the camp meeting at Lake Brady, and for the Saginaw Valley Spiritualists. He was even nominated for mayor of Grand Rapids in 1892. His wife, Sarah, died in 1917. Luther followed in 1919.

WILLIAM F. NYE

William F. Nye was born in Sandwich, Massachusetts in 1824 to Ebenezer and Sevena Nye. He moved to New Bedford when he was 16 to learn carpentry. After marrying Mary Skeith in 1851, he traveled to California during the gold rush where he worked for a contractor, returning home about 1855. He enlisted and served in the Civil War as a member of the Massachusetts cavalry. After he returned home in 1865, he began a small business refining oil. He sold the finest watch and sewing machine oil in the world and traveled widely for his business. William was a prominent Spiritualist, helping found the Onset camp. He died at the age of 86 in 1910.

JAMES M. PEEBLES

James M. Peebles was born in 1822 in Whitingham, Vermont, the oldest of seven children. According to a biography written by Edward Whipple in 1901, "From early childhood this boy was magnetic, genial, benevolent, and witty, but stubborn and capricious withal."

James was educated in a little red schoolhouse. He had a serious speech impediment, but a Professor Hurlburt helped him get over his stammer. When he was about 12, the family moved to Smithville, New York where they struggled to make ends meet. James did well with his schooling and was active in the Literary Society and Debating School. He taught a portion of the year to pay for his own schooling. After graduating at 16, he taught school in Picher, New York.

James questioned the teachings of traditional religion and searched for a belief system that wasn't harsh and judgmental. The Universalists church was just beginning. James saw a flier posted by Rev. N. Doolittle. and joined the church. He continued teaching and pursued his own education, including studying languages and medicine and eventually theology. He was only 20 years old when he became a reverend.

During the last year of his pastorate in Kelloggsville, New York in 1845, he was invited by the Hon. Vincent Kenyon to ride to Auburn and hear the spirit rappings. James was impressed and began to read about other religious teachings like those of Swedenborg.

James married Mary M. Conkey in 1850. They had three children who died in childhood and the marriage did not last. In 1856, James accepted a pastorate in Baltimore at the Universalist Society, but the call of Spiritualism was not far behind. During 1853-55, he was pastor of the Universalist Church at Elmira, NY. But he was not happy with their beliefs and questioned his own. He eventually resigned and became

162

acquainted with medium Charles Dunn who became his traveling companion in his Spiritualist ministry.

In 1861, James left for San Diego, California where he introduced himself to Rev. A. C. Edmunds, editor of *The Star of the Pacific*, a Universalist publication. James wrote several articles for Edmunds and reported his experiences to the *Herald of Progress*. He also lectured throughout the state. He eventually returned to Battle Creek, Michigan a year later. Through Dunn and others, he contacted a very ancient band of spirits who directed his actions. He lectured throughout much of the country, and became editor of *Banner of Light* in 1866.

James opened the Peebles' Institute of Health in Battle Creek, Michigan. He advertised that if one would send in their money and symptoms, he would mail them a diagnosis and cures. In 1903, the *Detroit Free Press* published news of his conviction in the case illegal use of the U.S. Mail in a psychic healing business.

Despite his business problems, James published over a dozen books and many articles. Emma Hardinge wrote "By his scholarly writings, and indefatigable labors as a lecturer, Mr. Peebles has been a gigantic lever in moving public opinion in favor of spiritual belief, and the repudiation of the effete superstition of old orthodoxy. Being a writer, an author, a graceful and accomplished orator, Mr. Peeble's services are in eager demand throughout the whole community...." He extended himself and traveled the world three times.

In his later years, Peebles divided his time between Battle Creek and Los Angeles. He died in California of a heart valve failure in 1922, just 36 days before his 100th birthday.

GEORGE F. AND EMALINE PERKINS

George Perkins was born in 1852 to Henry and Martha Perkins of Worcester, Massachusetts. He married Emiline Silvers, who was born in 1850 in New Jersey, in 1880. During the 1990s, the Perkins were active in the Spiritualist community. George gave lectures in Boston and Chicago in 1891 and the next year he was joined by Emaline in Brooklyn, New York. At Maple Dell Camp it was stated that their participants included, "Brother George Perkins, musical director, speaker and test medium, and his good wife, who is also a good clairvoyant and test medium."

In 1892, George published a new song book, *The Spiritual Evangelist,* that was "full of catchy melodies and appropriate hymns, for Spiritual meetings and circles." By 1895, both George and Emaline were well-known platform test-mediums who traveled through the northeastern United States, including Washington, D.C.

At the 7th annual national Spiritualists' convention in Chicago, George was listed as musical director, a Spiritualist missionary and worked as an usher during the meeting. The *Progressive Thinker,* 28 October 1899, wrote, "I wish to say a word in commendation of Geo. F. Perkins, one of the most faithful and exemplary workers in this city, a man who stands without reproach and who is always faithful in the discharge of every duty that confronts him." The article added, "Everyone who knows him and his wife knows there are no more faithful and conscientious laborers in the field, and also know that behind their mediumship is the element of character which is sometimes lacking in the more pretentious."

During the late 1890s, Rev. George F. Perkins and Rev. Emaline Perkins led the Beacon of Light Spiritualist Church in Chicago. Two of

166

their lecture topics were: "By Their Fruits Shall Ye Know Them" and "The Light of the World is Spirit."

The Perkins moved west in 1900. In 1901, George was listed as a singer, lecturer, and medium at the California state convention in San Francisco. Emeline passed in April of 1904 in San Francisco, and George resumed his lecture meetings at Odd Fellows Hall later that year. In 1905, he spoke and gave readings several times at the Union Spiritual Society in Oakland, presenting lectures on topics such as: "The Divine Three of the Origin of the Holy Trinity" and "Character."

In 1906, George wrote to the *Oakland Tribune*, 25 Nov 1906, "Don't you think the evangelists Simpson and Hibbard, at the Advent tent on Broadway, are over-stepping the boundary line of propriety and courtesy when they nightly abuse in the most emphatic language everybody and any organization that does not come under their particular endorsement? For weeks these men have used up all the dictionaries searching for words to express their contempt for every other religious denomination, more particularly the Roman Catholic and Spiritualists. And the President of the United States and our government do not escape their vitriolic tongues. Everyone has a right to advocate his conception of the truth and principles as set forth in the Bible, but I question any one's right to insult and abuse all who do not conscientiously agree with them on these puzzling questions."

George lived until at least 1930, when he was listed as a retired widower living in a rooming house in Oakland, California.

Rev. Tillie U. Reynolds

Matilda Upham was the only child born to Nathan and Mary Upham in 1841, at Sand Lake, New York. Nathan was a farmer at that time. By 1870, the family had moved to Troy, New York and Nathan worked as a U.S. Mail agent for the Hudson River Railroad. Matilda (Tillie) was already married, and she and her husband Newton Reynolds lived in the same house as her parents. Newton was a sign painter and Tillie a housekeeper.

Tillie's husband died in December of 1887, and she remained a widow, living alone in Troy, New York. It is not clear when Tillie's interest in Spiritualism began. In 1895, she was an established medium, holding seances at the Psychical Hall in Glens Falls, New York. During October, 1895 she "was controlled by several spirits, and her discourses were highly edifying. The psychometeric tests were mystifying and satisfactory in their results," according to *The Post-Star*, 25 October 1895. In a following article on November 4th, the paper said, "Mrs. Tillie U. Reynolds concluded her month's engagement at Psychic Hall, with two very interesting inspirational lectures yesterday afternoon and evening. Both lectures were followed by psychometric readings, which were well received by the audience, nearly if not all of the tests given being promptly recognized. During her sojourn here Mrs. Reynolds has drawn large audiences, and the gentle and kindly spirit in which she has taught the philosophy of the survival of the soul, has not only proved very attractive, but has also made for her many friends among those who, up to this time of her present visit have taken no interest whatever in psychic phenomena."

Tillie maintained a long list of speaking engagements and public demonstrations for over 30 years. She made appearances at Spiritualist camps: Lake Pleasant in Massachusetts, Queen City in Vermont, and Lily Dale in New York. In 1898, she was a speaker at the International Jubilee in Rochester, New York, and delegate for the sixth convention of the National Spiritualists' Association in Washington, D.C. She was chosen for the 1899 Invocation at the Convention of New York State Association of Spiritualists and Brooklyn Spiritualist Society. At that event she said, "We lay the foundations for a church that will be larger than any now established. We are not forcing our religion upon anyone; we only offer it to those who are hungry and long for enlightenment. We are the only ones that know immortality is true," according to *The Standard Union*, Brooklyn, 18 January 1899. She drew a large crowd when she lectured at Psychic Hall in November of 1899. Her talks were entitled, "When the World is Free" and "Death and Immortality."

Tillie was praised in President Harvey W. Richardson's report of the New York State Spiritualist Association published in *The Sunflower*, 24 June 1905. Richardson said, "I could not devote the usual amount of time to state work, and much of that would naturally devolve upon the president has fallen upon the shoulders of our second vice president, Mrs. Tillie Reynolds, to whose untiring efforts as State Missionary and Lyceum Superintendent, together with these added burdens of relieving the president, is very largely due whatever success in State Association work we have to our credit." Tillie had gone above and beyond with her missionary work, spreading the word about Spiritualism. She had worked tirelessly to increase interest in lyceum work throughout the state. She was also on the finance committee.

In 1915, she was listed in the monthly magazine, *The Spiritualist*, as Reverend Tillie Reynolds, an inspirational lecturer and message bearer. That same year she had a two-week engagement at Psychic Hall with the First Psychical Society in Glens Falls, New York. In 1916, she was elected vice president for the New England Spiritualist Camp Meeting Association at Lake Pleasant, Massachusetts. By 1920, she was living in Rochester with her niece, Harriet Brawer. She was a state missionary, director of the general assembly, and assistant pastor of Plymouth Spiritualist Church of Rochester before she passed in 1924.

HONORABLE ALMON B. RICHMOND

Almon B. Richmond was born in Indiana in 1825, the youngest child of Lawton and Sarah Richmond. He was a direct descendant of John Richmond, a Puritan who arrived on the Mayflower. His father was a physician and surgeon whose practice extended throughout the countryside. After the family moved to Chautauqua, New York, Almon attended Allegheny College, first taking medical courses and then studying law in Meadville, Pennsylvania.

He was admitted to practice in 1851 and had a long law career as a defense attorney, practicing in several states. *The History of Crawford County* published in 1885, states that he was involved in 4,000 criminal cases, 65 of which were homicides. By the time he retired in 1903, he had been involved with over 100 homicide cases.

Along with law, Almon was well versed in mechanics and the sciences. He was appointed assistant director of machinery at Crystal Palace in 1853. He also gave many lectures on philosophy, physiology, and chemistry. He was an advocate of the Temperance Movement and delivered many lectures on the topic. His books included *Leaves from the Diary of an Old Lawyer*, *Intemperance and Crime*, and *Court and Prisoner*.

Almon visited Cassadaga Lake (Lily Dale today) in 1887 and became interested in Spiritualism. He later wrote books entitled *A Review of the Seybert Commissioner's Report* and *Nemesis of Chautauqua Lake or Circumstantial Evidence*, a fictional story. In the introduction, he writes: "Fiction is often truth colored by the brush or pen of the artist, or molded by the chisel of the sculptor."

During the 1890s he was a regular lecturer at Cassadaga Lake and researched psychic phenomena and occult sciences. According to the *Record-Argus*, 19 July 1906, "He also lectured on many subjects and was for several years one of the most attractive personalities on the Spiritualistic lecture platform." He also authored: "What I saw at Cassadaga."

A lecture given by Almon at the Meadville Psychological Hall in 1889 entitled "The Dual Life; or, the Natural and the Spiritual Body" attracted a large crowd. He began by stating that the natural and spiritual body are in sympathy with each other. *The Evening Republican* reported that he said: "The belief that there is no hereafter is disloyalty to truth and treason to science." It continued: "In telling what spiritualism has done and is doing, the essayist, among other things, said it confirms the faith of the Christian, and ignores the dark superstition of a hell."

Almon published articles in the 1891 book, *Golden Way*. He wrote in his "Immortality" article, "If there is a spirit world, and if the spirits of those who have 'passed away' can and do visit the scenes of their earthly life they must all be governed by the laws that environ them in their new existence, and although any one may invoke their presence it is not certain that they will always come at their bidding. For this reason, set investigations by learned and honest committees may fail in obtaining results as satisfactory as those of the private séance or home circle."

Almon retired from practice and moved to Pittsburgh in 1903 where he died at the home of his son three years later in 1906.

CORA L. V. SCOTT

Cora Lodencia Veronica Scott was born near Cuba, New York in 1840. When she reached the age of twelve, while her family was living in Waterloo, Wisconsin, Cora began falling into trances and channeling spirits. Her parents, who were Universalists, had an interest in Spiritualism. They began to tour locally, sharing Cora's talents as a trance lecturer and healer.

Cora's spirit guides directed her to drop out of school when she was only twelve years of age. She channeled a German Physician for about four years, making many remarkable cures. After that time, her central guide became a young Native American girl named Ouina.

Cora's father died in 1853 and the following year she moved to Buffalo, New York. Cora and Ouina came to the attention of Professor J. J. Mapes of New York City while he was investigating Spiritualism. Cora's ability to heal had stopped about this time, but she focused on her lectures, which now covered a variety of topics about which she knew nothing. Mapes tested her by choosing the topic, Primary Rocks. He was so impressed by Cora's understanding of the subject that he said, "I am a college educated man, and have been all my life an investigator of scientific subjects and associated with scientific men, but I stand here this afternoon dumb before this young girl."

Cora married the first of her four husbands, Benjamin Franklin Hatch, at the age of 16. The 46-year-old mesmerist acted as her manager and promoted her around the country. He charged large fees for each public appearance, making huge profits. Hatch had their audiences form committees to propose questions and topics for the spirit lectures, to ensure Cora had not prepared for the subject matter. She also entered debates while in trance and answered any questions posed to her.

Cora was not always able to discuss a topic with accuracy. In 1857, in Lynn, Massachusetts, a committee reported: "Resolved, That we, the citizens of Lynn, who have listened to the exposition of Mrs. C. L. V. Hatch this evening, feel it our duty to say to the public that, in our opinion, she has failed to comply with any test which could have been reasonably expected from the wording of the call, or to give evidence of any supernatural inspiration; and we feel called upon to warn our fellow-citizens against her impositions."

Cora sued for divorce in 1858, citing abuse, but didn't go through with it. Rumors suggested Hatch was visiting prostitutes. He later sued her for divorce in 1863, accusing Cora of adultery. After a bitter battle that played out in the courts and the press, the divorce was final. Cora's second husband may have had the surname, Daniels, but there are no details available.

Cora's third marriage was to Samuel Forster Tappan, an abolitionist, Native American rights activist, and military officer. The Tappans lived in Washington, D.C. where Cora was one of Lincoln's advisers. She also worked with President Andrew Johnson and President Ulysses Grant. Who presented her with a *Resolution of Gratitude* for her six years of service.

Her marriage to Samuel Tappan ended in divorce and Cora moved to England in 1873. It was estimated that she gave three thousand lectures during her three-year visit. When she returned to the United States, she married William Richmond and moved to Chicago. He published several of her books. Her publications included: *The Soul: Its Nature, Relations and Expressions in Human Embodiments* (1888), *Psychosophy, in Six Parts* (1915), and *My Experiences While Out of Body and My Return After Many Days* (1923).

Cora continued with her trance lectures. In 1883, she gave a message to the nation from Washington, D.C. by channeling President James A.

Garfield. In 1892 she officiated at the funeral of Henrietta S. Maynard, Lincoln's medium.

Cora was one of the founding members of the National Spiritualist Association in 1893, becoming the first Vice President. She opened the First Society of Spiritualists in Chicago. Audience numbers ranged from 2000-5000 and increasing interest forced her to keep looking for bigger venues. The church later became known as the Church of the Soul.

Cora died on in 1923 after serving Spiritualism for over 70 years.

JAMES RILEY

James Riley was born in Philadelphia in 1843, one of five children. After their mother died, their father, a foreman at a boiler works, put them into the care of a neighboring family because he needed to travel for work. Eventually, the families moved to Cass County, Michigan, where his father bought a farm.

James showed a gift for clairvoyance when he was only three years old. He knew many child spirits who considered him as a playmate. At one point, one of the spirits materialized to him. When he was around seven, James began table tipping. The demonstrations became so popular, he was invited to neighboring farms to show his abilities. During one séance, three big men couldn't hold the table in place.

James' father put a stop to the table tipping, and James went back to a more normal life. At the age of 13, he worked for other farmers in the Michigan area. When the Civil War broke out in 1861, he enlisted in the 42nd Illinois Infantry and participated in many battles during his almost four-year stint in the army. He married Martha Nicols in 1865, and they had seven children who lived.

Disillusioned with traditional Christian religion, James claimed to be an agnostic in 1885. At about the same time, he visited a Spiritualist camp at Lake Cora, Van Buren County, in southwestern Michigan. He met medium Charles Barnes, who brought messages from an army buddy, Jeff Boyd. James was so impressed that he and Martha tried conducting seances in their own home.

They tried for six months. Vlerebome, A. (1911) in *The Life of James Riley Commonly Called Farmer Riley* wrote, " ...the force was undeserved by the boy and yet manifested; was earnestly deserved by the man, yet failed to make itself known."

Finally, one night after sitting for three hours, James suggested that they quit for the evening. Martha said that they had nothing better to do, why not sit a little longer. The table moved for the first time. Then the spirit of Martha' brother Ezra, who had died in the war in 1864, came to them.

James realized that connecting with the spirit world was not something a person could command. The spirits were using him and would work on their own timetable. After that realization, messages came to them through rapping. People traveled from miles around to see Farmer Riley. He successfully used slate writing at his daughter Emma's house.

In 1886 or 1887, John Benton became James' spirit guide. James would sit in a cabinet in the darkness. Those attending the séance would sing hymn's until spirits materialized. These spirits were usually men clad in older evening dress fashions.

While James conducted seances, he continued to question the "whys" of things. He concluded that death was just a change, "a dropping away of the physical body." He saw man as a progressive creature who continued to develop after moving into the spirit world. Hell was not a location; it was a condition of the spirit. For that reason, spirits were separated into different grades which represented their point of development. Just as people learn on Earth, they also do in heaven.

Martha Riley died in 1903, but James Riley's date of death is unknown.

FRANK T. RIPLEY

Frank T. Ripley was born in Bath, Maine in 1848 to shoemaker Edward Ripley and his wife, Asenath. There is little information on his life, but he made Boston his homebase while he journeyed across the country for thirty years representing Spiritualism as a test medium.

By 1880, he was listed as a travelling trance and public test medium in Spiritualist publications. His engagements took him throughout the northeastern portion of the country in the 1880s, with him gradually moving westward as Spiritualism flourished. In 1881, he reached Wisconsin and Colorado. By 1890, he was a regular speaker and medium for the Boston Spiritual Temple Society while he was in town.

At an engagement in Rindge, New Hampshire, "Mr. Ripley's tests were marvelous in their correctness, and were the theme of the conversation all over the grounds." In 1892, he spent a month in Wonewoc, Wisconsin and recruited 50 people to join the Wonewoc Spiritual Association. The same year he travelled to St. Paul. M. T. C. Flower, president of The Alliance, in the *Banner of Light*, 7 May 1892, wrote, "That he is a remarkable platform test medium goes without saying, as thousands of people can testify who have witnessed his public tests given from the rostrum at close of his lectures, and at the weekly test circles given in aid of the society."

Frank's travels took him to New Orleans, Grand Rapids, and as far west as California. In 1887 in Los Angeles, he was called "one of the greatest mediums of the present age." The *Los Angeles Herald* wrote, "Mr. Ripley is a large hearted, whole souled man, one who at once inspires confidence in his hearers, and as he has been in such great demand throughout the eastern states, being engaged for months ahead, our association considers itself very fortunate in securing the services of Mr.

Ripley. Each service will consist of a short inspirational address upon 'The Philosophy of Spiritualism' and after the address demonstrations of the same by giving his wonderful and convincing tests."

In *The Courier-Journal* (Louisville, Kentucky), 16 February 1900, Rev. Dr. Frank T. Ripley was described as "the oldest test medium on the American platform. He spoke but a few moments, telling of the comfort he had derived from the teachings of spiritualism and from the feeling that when his friends passed away they would still be able to communicate with him In closing he said that he had learned that the future spiritual world would be material like the present world, but in it everything would be more refined and much purer."

Frank's life appeared to be a solitary one. There is no record of a wife or family. In 1900, in Allen, Indiana, he was listed as a single boarder. His life revolved around Spiritualism and his lectures included a 1910 talk in Buffalo entitled: "Spirit World Life and Labor There" and 1914 Elmira, New York lectures including "After Death, What?" and "What Shall I Do to Be Saved?"

Frank died in Jamestown, New York in 1914 after giving a lecture and readings. He was buried by the Masons because no family could be found.

JONATHAN M. ROBERTS

Jonathan M. Roberts was born in Montgomery County, Pennsylvania in 1821 to Jonathan and Eliza Roberts. His father was elected to the State Senate and then went on to the United States Congress from 1811-1814. Unfortunately, Jonathan's father died in 1854, six months before Jonathan married Mary Abbot. They went on to have six daughters over the next twenty years after moving to New Jersey.

Because of his father's success, Jonathan received a fine education and then studied law. Prior to the Civil War he was an active Abolitionist and became one of the leaders of the Republican party. He was frequently referred to as "General" or "Colonel." He may have played some role in the Civil War and made his fortune as a manufacturer of cast-iron stoves.

Jonathan became a believer of Spiritualism about 1873 when he was put in contact with the spirit of his father. That belief was solidified when James A. Bliss brought forth his deceased daughter. By 1878, he started publishing and editing *Mind and Matter* with C.C. Wilson and James A Bliss as a weekly journal that covered the interests of Spiritualism.

Jonathan may have been too enthralled with Spiritualists and mediums to hold them under critical analysis. His journal became a place to attack the *Religio-Philosophical Journal* (which tended to publish criticisms of mediums' frauds), and featured accounts of mediums who had shown themselves to be frauds. He also used his law background to sue others for defaming him or criticizing his proteges. He even sued on behalf of Alfred James after James had signed an affidavit that he had been cheating. Jonathan also defended mediums such as Madame Blavatsky and the Holmes materializing mediums, suing a Philadelphia newspaper for defamation.

Jonathan's interest in free thought led him to oppose "Christian spiritualism." He argued that Christ was really Apollonius and Christianity really Buddhism, and that both had been delivered by the spirits and then perverted by the priests of the early church. His publications included, *Antiquity Unveiled: Ancient Voices from the Spirit Realms Proving Christianity to be of Heathen Origin* and *Apollonius of Tyana, Identified as the Christian Jesus.*

Jonathan died in 1888 at his home in Burlington, New Jersey at the age of 67 after being stricken with paralysis for several weeks. An article in *The Philadelphia Times*, 1 March 1888, stated that "He defended the faith of his adoption with great energy, which led him into many legal difficulties and, it is said, was the indirect cause of his death."

Mrs. Anna L. Robinson

Anna Dutter was born to Peter and Lucinda Dotter in Portage County, Ohio about 1855. Her father passed away in 1860. Anna married Rosco Manchester in 1872 and they had two sons before moving to Deerfield, Michigan where Rosco oversaw a livery stable. Anna was a housewife.

The couple ended their relationship during the 1880s. By 1890, Anna was going by the name Mrs. Anna L. Robinson. She was very active as a lecturer and medium in the Spiritualist community, attending the Mantua Springs and Haslett Park summer camps. Her 1893 Hazlett Park Camp meeting address was entitled: "Concentration of Thought and Forces and Spiritual Development."

Anna moved to Port Huron, Michigan in 1893 where she became pastor of the United Progressive Club. The Port Huron *Times Herald*, 22 November 1893, published United Progressive Club resolutions in her honor. One being, "That we will ever cherish with suspect, love and affection, the memory of Mrs. Anna L. Robinson, who has brought joy to so many sorrowing hearts, with loving, tender messages from spirit friends, and who has so long and so faithfully labored for the cause of humanity and truth, and the upbuilding of all those principles which elevate and beautify our lives, bringing us nearer to the Angel-world, and enlarging our sphere of usefulness among our fellows."

In the 24 February 1894, *Progressive Thinker*, Stuart L. Rogers wrote: "I wish to inform the Spiritualists that my opinion of Sister Anna. L Robinson, of Port Huron, Mich., is that she is a superior instrument in the hands of the angels. I have had some demonstrations through her that are very correct. I am an old investigator of the spiritual philosophy, and my opportunities have been very good." Mrs. Robinson's spirit contact was named Alice. Others commented on her elegance and ability to attract large audiences.

Anna's popularity increased. She established a Band of Mercy with 60 members and attended the state association in 1894. She lectured and was a test medium at Catalpa Camp in Liberal, Missouri in 1894 and became Vice President of the camp the following year. In the 18 May 1895, edition of *Light of Truth,* a personal story about one of her readings was published in detail.

Anna married Jerimiah S. Gillespie in Port Huron in 1899 and attended Camp Chesterfield in Indiana and Lily Dale the same year. The Muncie *Morning News,* 28 July 1899, quoted part of her lecture, "I believe we often make mistakes in our prayers. We most always pray for a happy time in the spirit world. Would it not be better to pray: 'Oh, guiding Spirit, help us to know how to make ourselves happy here and now?' Do not ask God to forgive our sins, but let us learn how not to commit them, for cause is always followed by its legitimate effect. Let us not cry, 'Warehouse man what of the night?' but what of the day, of this day, of every day." She continued, "Yes, Spiritualism is the truth, investigate and enjoy it, but always hold your own spirit intact. Get all you can from your spirit teachers and then sift through your own mental sieve."

By 1900, Anna and Jeremiah Gillespie were living in Oakland, California with her two sons and an adopted daughter. Gillespie was Secretary of the *Philosophical Journal* published in San Francisco and President of the California State Spiritualists Association. Anna was pastor of the People's Church in San Francisco and continued to attend Spiritualist camps across the country, including Camp Brady and Camp Chesterfield.

Later in her life, Anna returned to Michigan and became pastor of the Spiritualist Church in Battle Creek. Her 1926 obituary stated that she was one of the "best known workers among spiritualistic circles in the United States and Canada." She was "actively associated with the Lily Dale spiritualistic camp in New York State and National Superintendent of the Lyceums of the United States and Canada."

Dr. Fred Schermerhorn

Fred Schermerhorn was born in 1856 to farmers, Cornelius and Sarah Schermerhorn, in LaMont, Michigan, the eldest of their three children. He married Janette (Nettie) Thornton in 1880 and, by the late 1880s, was a well-known physician and medium in the Spiritualist community. He was listed as a lecturer and clairvoyant psychometrist and became Secretary of State of Michigan Spiritualists.

The *Religio-philosophical Journal,* vol 44, no 6, March 31, 1888, published an article about Harry E. Millard testing Fred at five different circles. The article discusses Millard's testing protocol which included binding the doctor's hands and arms and checking for various ways he could deceive the group. Millard wrote, "If these manifestations were not the result of spirit force (as it was impossible to be trickery of the Doctor), will some scientist please unravel the mystery and tell me what caused them? "

Fred's notoriety increased. In 1891, he wrote from his home in Rochester to the *Progressive Thinker,* "I am speaking to crowded houses every Sunday night, and the cause so dear to our hearts is rapidly gaining ground here." In 1893, the First Spiritualist Society of Muskegon was organized and Fred ran the services for four weeks. Over the next few years, he attended Haslett Park Spiritualist Camp where he gave lectures and tests, attended the Saginaw Valley Spiritual Association meeting at Owosso where he gave an address at the symposium "Spiritualism as a Religion, Science and Philosophy," and lectured at the Benton Harbor, Michigan State Spiritual Association meeting while he was Secretary of the organization.

In 1895, he ran an ad in the *Banner of Light* that stated: "Magnetic Institute of Psychometry. A rare offer. Send lock of hair, name, age, sex, one leading symptom, and 6 cents in stamps, and get a free diagnosis and psychometric reading by spirit power. F. Schermerhorn, MD, Manager, Graduate of Michigan State University, 74 Bostwick street, Grand Rapids, Mich."

Fred moved to Ohio and was active in the community, conducting a meeting at the Ohio State Convention in 1897 and a meeting in Lima, Ohio the same year. Rev. Moses Hull, who ran a homiletic school in Mantua, Ohio, wrote in *The Light of Truth*, 19 June 1897, "While there is at this school a dearth of young men and women who stand in the most need of the instruction to be imparted, we are glad to welcome to our classes such able workers as Dr. Schermerhorn and his good and talented wife. Though the doctor holds a diploma from Michigan university, and, I believe, from some theological institution, as well, he is strongly of the opinion that no man can know too much., so he has enrolled and is at work hard as a student."

Fred and his wife moved to Montrose, Colorado in 1898. He was a practicing physician and surgeon, charter member of the original Montrose Lions club, President and District Governor of Lions International and city coroner. He was also a State Senator from 1912-1924.

Fred died at the age of 91 in 1947 following a long illness. His obituary in the *Daily Sentinel* stated that "The physician was an active member of civic clubs and fraternal organizations and was widely known over the western slope of Colorado and throughout the state." There was no mention of Spiritualism.

MRS. ABIGAIL E. SHEETS

Abigail E. Sheets was born in 1848 to carpenter/farmer Martin B. and Eliza Ann Sheets in Madison, Ohio, being one of their three children. She married Albert Cogswell in 1863, and they had a son Henry by 1865. They were living in Otsego, Michigan by 1870, but the marriage did not last. Albert and Abigail divorced by 1875 when Albert married Mary Ann Perry.

In 1880, Abigail was a dressmaker living in Lansing, Michigan. Both she and her family were involved with Spiritualism. In 1881, her father, Martin, was known as a professor of clairvoyance and magnetism in town. Abigail worked at Camp Onset in the late 1880s. In 1895, her father, Mr. M. B. Sheets of Grand Ledge, judged an essay writing contest entitled: "What Good Has Spiritualism Done," which was published in the *Progressive Thinker*.

By 1891, the Sheets family were living in Grand Ledge, a well-known Spiritualist camp. Abigail was listed as Mrs. Abbie E. Sheets, medium, for the 1893 First National Delegate Convention of Spiritualists of the United States in Chicago. She was also a trustee at Haslett Park Camp. In 1895 and 1896, she was Vice President of the Michigan State Spiritualist Association and President of the Grand Ledge Spiritualist Camp Association from 1894 until 1904.

The *Banner of Light*, 14 November 1896, published a summary of her talk at the Boston Spiritual Temple entitled: "What can you tell of reincarnation?" During her talk, she said, "In this sense we may feel that we have lived before. But though we passed to spirit-life many centuries ago from the far-away land of the Orient, in all our journeyings through the higher realms we have never met a spirit that proved to our satisfaction that he ever lived in a human body upon the earth-plane but once in his march from the lower to the higher kingdom. If other spirits have lived upon the earth-plane many times we have not learned of the fact to our satisfaction."

The late 1890s were a busy time for Abigail. She lectured and gave public addresses at Grand Ledge; Lake Helen, Florida; and the Michigan state convention in 1897. She was a state delegate at the convention the following year.

Abigail's father died in 1898 at Grand Ledge, but she and her mother remained there. Her lectures continued with engagements at the Owosso, Michigan Spiritualist Society and at Sturgis, Michigan at the Free or Spiritualist Church. In 1903, she spoke in Indianapolis. When she attended the 1908 Grand Ledge Spiritualist Camp, the following was published: "The opening week Mrs. Abbie Sheets filled the entire week's engagements giving her highly Spiritual addresses to the entire satisfaction of her listeners."

Abigail spoke to the Lansing First Society of Spiritualists and officiated funeral services. By 1910, she was living alone at Grand Ledge and eventually moved to California to be near her son. She died in 1915 in Glendale, California and was buried near her ex-husband, Albert, who died in 1914 and her son, Henry, who died in 1925. A Michigan obituary said, "Mrs. Abbie Sheets for 30 years a resident of this city, until she went to California, last August, passed away Saturday at the home of her son, Henry Cogswell."

MRS. ALTHEA C. SMITH

Althea (Elithea) Clarissa Blood was born in 1829 to Jonas and Hopey Blood in New Hampshire. She married Benjamin F. Smith, and they had a son, Charles, in 1847. By 1870, Althea and Benjamin were living in Lawrence, Massachusetts where Benjamin worked in a wool mill.

In the *Banner of Light,* 29 September 1888, the publication announced that they reopened their séance room with Althea being one of their mediums. "On Friday afternoon this circle-room will be open, as formerly, for the presentation of spirit messages through the organism of Mrs. B. F. Smith. The spiritual intelligences interested in this work are gathered here in perfect harmony, ready to give forth the best of their power and labor for the dissemination of truth and the assistance of spirits who desire to reach their mortal friends."

Althea had a column of her readings in the *Banner of Light* under her married name, Mrs. B. F. Smith, from about 1888-1896. At that time, she lived at Vernon Cottage, Crescent Beach, Revere, Massachusetts. Readings were transcribed during the circles held Friday afternoons and about a half-dozen were published in each issue.

The *Banner of Light,* 26 October 1889, published the following announcement. "Free Spiritual meeting. These highly interesting meetings, to which the public is cordially invited, are held at the Hall at the Banner of Light Establishment. On Tuesdays and Fridays at 8:00 pm. Mrs. B. F. Smith, the excellent test medium, will on Friday afternoons, under the influence of her guides give decarnated individuals an opportunity to send words of love to their earthly friends—which messages are reported at considerable expense and published each week in The Banner."

Althea was listed as a medium in 1890 in Spiritualist publications and gave private readings at her home. In 1891, she advertised in the *Banner of Light*. "Mrs. B. F. Smith, Trance Medium sittings at Vernon Cottage, Crescent Beach Revere Mass. Friday, Saturday and Sunday, from 9-6."

Her husband, Benjamin, had severe illness that began in December of 1891. He died the following year. Althea continued with her work as a medium and by giving inspirational talks and addresses at funerals. In 1894, she gave an inspirational address at the funeral of Dr. Charles Main.

In the 8 September 1894 issue of the *Banner of Light*, they published some of the "thank you" letters sent to Althea. The *Banner* wrote, "The good words corroborative of the reliability of spirit-communications in The Banner, and high praise for the excellent mediumship of Mrs. B.F. Smith, continue to pour in upon us."

In the *Boston Post*, 4 February 1894, they featured Spiritualism and republished four messages given by Mrs. B. F. Smith that had been listed in the *Banner of Light*. Althea continued giving messages for the Banner until 1896. She died in 1911 at her house on Beach Street in Revere at the age of 82.

DR. EZRA A. AND FANNIE DAVIS SMITH

Ezra A. Smith was influential in establishing the Queen City Park Spiritualist camp. He was born in 1839, one of four children of John and Elvira Grisworld Smith in Pittsford, Vermont. In 1850, he lived with the Griswold family. He graduated from Dartmouth College and, by 1860, was listed as a physician. Fannie Davis was born in 1839 in Massachusetts. She married Ezra in 1861 in Milford, Massachusetts, and they made their home in Brandon, Vermont. They had no children.

Fannie was a well-known public speaker in both Massachusetts and New York City. According to her obituary in *The Brandon Union,* 20 October 1893, "The anti-slavery cause and every other great movement and spiritual elevation of the masses received her loyal and effective support." She dedicated herself to public work for 32 years, and "established the truths of spiritualism." She was an associate of Wendall Phillips, William Lloyd Garrison, and Henry C. Wright.

Ezra was the first President of the Queen City Park Association from 1882 to 1899, as well as President of the Vermont State Spiritualist Society from 1898 to 1908. *The Burlington Clipper,* 2 July 1898 said, because of "his untiring zeal and effort and masterly executive and business ability a very large part of the success of the place is due."

JOSEPH D. STILES

Joseph D. Stiles was born in 1828 to Joseph and Lucy Stiles in Concord, Massachusetts. He was the only son of six children and raised in the Universalist church. In 1850, his sister Harriet discovered she was a table-tipping medium. While other members of the family became mediums, Joseph worked in the printing business at a Universalist newspaper. In 1853, he quit his job as type setter and attended several séance circles in Boston to develop his abilities which had suddenly come upon him.

Initially, Joseph began by acting as a conduit for the spirit of John Quincy Adams for Josiah Brigham in June of 1854 through spirit writing. Brigham recognized Adams' handwriting in the first letter, which was dated 9 July 1854. From then on, Stiles began to produce messages in notebooks from Adams. The messages ended in March 1857, and they produced a publication of all the messages entitled *Twelve Messages*.

Joseph moved to Weymouth, Massachusetts where he became a platform medium by falling into trances under the guidance of a Native American spirit named Swift Arrow. He filled halls in various New England towns with large audiences. He also attended camps, seances and conventions. In 1867, he spent several months in Vermont delivering messages from spirits named Hosea Ballou, Theodore Parker, and war heroes Colonel Elmer Ellsworth and General Nathaniel Lyon.

In a biographical sketch published 7 July 1886 in *Facts* the editor wrote, "Mr. Stiles is an inspirational speaker, never attempting to prepare his lectures, and being naturally unassuming and retiring in nature, and as he has expressed himself to us, always fearful lest some time he might not succeed, he dreads to appear as a lecturer; but we have listened to some purely inspirational lectures given by him which, in matter and diction, we have seldom heard equaled or excelled."

At an 1884 conference at Lake Sunapee Spiritualist Camp, one hundred eighty-nine spirits identified themselves through Joseph in an hour and fifteen minutes. In *Medium and Daybreak*, 14 May 1886, J. J. Morse wrote, "Mr. Stiles is simply indescribable: names in full, Christian and sur, dates and incidents, localities and definite particulars, and long lists of family relationships, literally pour from him when entranced. On one occasion we heard him give 265 names, 263 of which, by actual count, were unhesitatingly identified."

The editor of *Spirit Voices*, 9 September 1885, wrote: "Swift Arrow, through his medium, Joseph D. Stiles, has given about nine tests of spirit-presence." At the National Development Circle, he gave 175 names of spirits that were recognized by the audience.

Joseph was a lifelong bachelor and died at his mother's home in Weymouth, Massachusetts in 1897 at the age of 68. His obituary in *The Boston Globe* wrote that he was "one of the most prominent Spiritualist test mediums and lecturers in the state...."

DR. HERMAN B. STORER

Herman Storer was born in New Haven, Connecticut in 1825 to William and Mary Storer. He began work as a printer and publisher and married his first wife, Sarah Butler, while living in New Haven. She died in 1849 at the young age of 21. Herman remarried to Emily Trowbridge. By 1865, they were living in Brooklyn, and he was working as a chemist. It's not clear when he became a physician, but he is listed as being one in the 1880 Boston census.

After he became a Spiritualist, Herman worked consistently, either as a medium, lecturer or healer. He was a Spiritualist for more than 50 years and very prominent in camp meeting work, especially during the 1870s and 1880s. He took an active role at Nickerson's Grove camp and later at Onset Bay. "He had a large clientele as a Spiritualist healer, but he did not wholly discard the use of medicine; much of it, however, he claimed to use under spirit direction. He was a broad and liberal minded man," according to the *Boston Globe*, 28 Dec 1896.

The *Boston Post*, 1 April 1895, published an article about Storer relating his conversion to Spiritualism to those attending the Boston Spiritual Temple on the 47th anniversary of modern Spiritualism: "The calendar indicates that we have made forty-seven stops on the spiritual highway, but the calendar does not indicate the progress made in public opinion since the dawn of modern spiritualism. I have been a spiritualist for forty-five years, and the joy and blessing of my life I attribute to this source.

"I began, as ignorance usually begins, by denying the manifestations. My friend, an editor of a country journal, had been down to Eliken Phelps' and published the wonderful manifestations said to have happened there. I sent out word to him that I would not attempt to build up my journal on the basis of sensational stories. He came in to see me,

216

and I saw that he was thoroughly convinced of the seances. At his invitation I went down to Stratford and called upon Dr. Phelps. I heard something in the front room. I went and looked. There the piano was being pushed from where it usually stood to where it now rests, and a piece of music came up and rested on the stand.

"I looked at the doctor. He had been a Congregational minister and was the picture of a reverend and reliable man. My house has been full of brother ministers and lawyers belonging to the family. They have been confounded and no evidence of anything, but spirit work has been discovered. I asked them if a medium could be found to give some more evidence. He mentioned Miss Brook, a girl of 13, at Bridgeport. I went down there at once and was invited to join the circle at her home in the evening. The circle began to ask silent questions, and though the raps came we were all ignorant, except the questioner, as to the responses. By and by it came my turn. I asked if there was any spirit that would communicate with me. At once the table was covered with raps.

"My first wife spelled out her maiden name and how long she had been in the spirit—less than two years. And then came a message spelling her baby's name. Facts followed facts, then my future mediumship was predicted, which after two years came true and has been with me ever since."

Dr. Herman Storer died the following year in April 1896 at the age of 71.

ALBERT E. TISDALE

Albert E. Tisdale was born about 1851 to Reuben and Jane Tisdale in Essex County, Massachusetts, one of their five children. By 1863, his mother was a widow in Norwich, Connecticut. Albert entered the Navy when he was only ten years of age by serving as an orderly to Commodore Ringgold on the frigate Sabine. Commodore Ringgold sent Albert home before the close of the Civil War to prepare for entrance to the naval academy. It was about this time that Albert began to have problems with his eyesight. In a short time, he became blind.

In 1880, Albert was still living at home with his mother, Jane, and his sister, Emma Bard, in Norwich, Connecticut. His interest in Spiritualism took hold about this time. In New London, *The Day*, 2 December 1884 published: "Albert E, Tisdale, who had the misfortune to lose his eyesight some 15 years ago, has blossomed out as an inspirational speaker. It is claimed that this spirit of a departed one named Denton controls the medium."

He became a well-known speaker, attending several Spiritualist camps in New England, including Lake Pleasant. He also lectured throughout Massachusetts, including in Boston and Springfield. In 1890, at Temple Heights, he sang songs before his lecture and gave readings afterward. He became known as the "Blind Medium of Merrick, Massachusetts." His lectures included topics such as: "The Human Family Knows No Greater Evil than War," "The Religion-Builders," "The Coming Struggle," "What is the Need of Jealousy among Mediums?" and "The Philosophy of Modern Spiritualism."

Albert also maintained his interest in the Navy. In the *Boston Globe*, 16 December 1894 he was listed as speaking before the Farragut Naval Veterans. "The next meeting of the association will take place

Wednesday evening, when an interesting lecture will be given by shipmate Albert E, Tisdale, the blind orator, the subject being, "The Cruise of U S Ship Sabine in Search of the Alabama, in the Fall and Winter of 1862-63."

Albert continued with his speaking engagements for the next two decades. The *Banner of Light,* 31 July 1897, wrote, "Mr. A. E. Tisdale was the next speaker, and was greeted with great applause. He spoke at length in regard to liberty, of religious shams and of the beauties of religion embodied in Modern Spiritualism; his remarks were received with hearty applause." He was a featured speaker at Golden Jubilee of Modern Spiritualism in Washington D. C, the same year.

At the 1898 Spiritualist camp meeting at Vicksburg he gave an inspirational address. "There never was a grander discourse delivered at this camp than the one furnished by his guides on this occasion." The *Lansing Journal,* 14 Feb 1901, printed, "Mr. Tisdale has been totally blind since childhood and is one of the most brilliant, profound and logical speakers on the spiritual platform. His addresses while entranced in connection with his singing and playing, make a most entertaining evening."

Albert died in Boston in 1906. *The Day,* 25 August 1906, of New London, wrote, "Albert E. Tisdale, a famous blind lecturer, once a resident of this city, was overcome by the heat in Boston Thursday and died in a few minutes. He had just arrived by steamer from Maine where he had been spending a vacation. Mr. Tisdale was known throughout New England as a lecturer and as the youngest naval veteran of the Civil War."

Fraternally
Hudson Tuttle

HUDSON AND EMMA ROOD TUTTLE

Hudson Tuttle was born in 1836 in Berlin Heights, Ohio, a member of an ardently religious family. He became dissatisfied with traditional religion when it didn't save him from beatings by his father. This led to an interest in other spiritual teachings. Spirit knockings popularized by the Fox Sisters were in the news at the time. Hudson decided to attend a seance hosted by a Congregational minister. He soon found he was able to enter a trance-like state and produce automatic writing as well as knocking.

During his trance states, Hudson communicated with spirit guides who relayed their knowledge to him. With only eleven months of elementary education, he would publish a large collection of books on a variety of topics, the contents of which he credited to his spirit guides. Charles Darwin referenced Hudson's book, *Origin and Antiquity of Physical Man*, in Chapter 7 of *The Descent of Man*.

Emma Rood was born in Braceville, Ohio. As a child, she was inspired by her grandfather's singing skills, which eventually led to her composing lyric poetry. Her father was a progressive man who followed news stories about the Poughkeepsie Seer and the rappings in Rochester. Even though he promised his wife to continue being a member of the Methodist church, he attended lectures on Spiritualism and séance circles.

Emma experienced the discrimination against Spiritualism when she attended Western Reserve Seminary. After one of her instructors said only "low class" people believed in such things, she left. It was her association with Madam Angelique Martin in her hometown that opened her to a world of new thoughts and ideas, including women's rights. Emma studied French, art, and painting with Madam Martin. At the age of seventeen, she began publishing poetry in the *Universe,* published in Cleveland.

The death of Emma's mother led to Emma's first experience with the spirit world, a disembodied trance-like state that enveloped her for nearly two weeks. It is not surprising, when she received a letter and book (*Life in Two Spheres*) from Hudson Tuttle in 1857 praising her poetry, that the two would end up marrying less than a year later when she was 18 years old.

Emma and Hudson were both prolific writers, lecturers and educators. Hudson's master work, *Arcana of Nature*, was published in 1909. It attempted to explain the origins of the cosmos and man by introducing astronomical, anthropological and philosophic concepts. His other works included *Scenes in the Spirit World* (1855), later published in England under the title *Life in Two Spheres, Career of Religious Ideas* (1878), *Religion of Man and Ethics of Science* (1890) and *Mediumship and its Laws* (1890).

Emma Rood raised their children, wrote poetry and journal articles, as well as collaborating with Hudson on books. Her earliest publications included *Blossoms of Our Spring* (1864), *Gazelle,* (1866), and *The Lyceum Guide* (1870). Her last book was *From Soul to Soul* (1890). Emma and Hudson co-wrote a book of spiritual folklore, *Stories from Beyond the Borderland* (1910).

In their co-written book, *A Golden Sheaf* (1907), they wrote, "There is only one attribute which goes forth always to return, bearing rich reward, and that is love. It is yielding as thinnest air, yet firm as adamant; it is gentle as the breath of the south wind, yet the strongest force in the universe; it looks backward as well as forward; reaches down to draw those below up to its vantage ground; reaches upward in its aspirations.

It is like the sun, which constantly pours out its flood of light and energy, giving all without expectancy of return."

Hudson Tuttle died in 1910, in Berlin Heights, Ohio. Emma followed in 1916. Both were committed Spiritualists who published actively on the subject.

CARRIE E. S. TWING

Caroline (Carrie) Edna Skinner was born in 1844 to Solomon and Candice Skinner of Sherman, Chautauqua County, New York. Solomon died in 1846 when Carrie and her sister were young girls, and their mother remained a widow. Carrie received a common school education and began teaching in the district schools when only seventeen years old. Afterward she attended the Westfield Academy and taught during the summers.

In 1871, Carrie married Herbert S. Twing, a bookkeeper turned vineyardist. They had a son Edward from his first marriage, and Carrie had a daughter, Candice, who was born in 1875 and died young. Carrie identified with the Spiritualist movement early in life. It's unclear how involved Herbert was with Spiritualism, but he was the business secretary at Camp Cassadaga in Florida in 1900.

In 1876, Carrie was mentioned in the *Boston Globe* as a mechanical writing medium. She attended Lake Pleasant Camp in Greenfield, Massachusetts the following year, working as a medium. By 1879, she was called a "celebrated test medium" at an event in Buffalo, New York.

During the 1880s she appeared at many northeastern locations, working as a test medium and giving private readings. The *Cleveland Leader and Morning Herald,* 6 April 1888, wrote "About one hundred persons paid twenty-five cents each to attend the public séance given by Mrs. Carrie E. S. Twing at Memorial Hall last evening. They enjoyed a privilege then which few could be more esteemed by a Cleveland audience—that of holding direct communication with Artemus Ward." Mr. Ward had been a humorist in the Cleveland area who wrote for the newspaper.

By the 1890s, Carrie regularly attended Lily Dale as a medium and speaker. She also authored several books, including *A Thrilling Account of the Late President Garfield's Reception in the Spirit World. Written through the hand of Carrie E. S. Twing, (1881); JIM, The Touch of an Angel Mother.* A psychic story (1905); *Lisbeth, A Story of Two Worlds; Henry Drummond in Spirit Life;* and *Golden Gleams from Heavenly Light.*

Carrie garnered a wide reputation as a lecturer and traveled extensively through the country. During the early 1900s, she attended Camp Cassadaga, lived for a time in Portland, Oregon, and attended Temple Heights and Lake Pleasant as well as Pine Grove Spiritualist Camps. In 1902, she was Vice President of the New York State Association of Spiritualists.

Carrie died in 1910, two years after her husband. The *Buffalo Courier*, 26 August 1910, wrote: "Mrs. Carrie E. S. Twing, the well-known lecturer, died at her home, a few miles southeast of this place today, after an illness of three weeks, from apoplexy. Mrs. Twing was taken ill in Boston while on a lecturing tour and was brought to her home here August 5th, lingering until now. Mrs. Twing frequently spoke at meetings of the granges.

"She was a speaker of much force, and had been heard throughout the middle, eastern and southern states. She was an authority on spiritualistic matters and a medium of acknowledged ability."

MRS. M. E. WALLACE

Mrs. M. E. Wallace is a bit of a mystery. She was born in 1855 in New York, was married eight years before being widowed, and had one child. Her child was presumably a daughter since her granddaughter's name was Lillie Moore.

In 1887, Mrs. Wallace was living at 219 W. 42nd Street in New York City. By that time, she was already active in Spiritualism. The *Banner of Light* reported she was Recording Secretary for The American Spiritualist Alliance and had meetings at her home with members: Mrs. Gridley, Dr. Wilson, Dr. Winn, Mrs. Beach, Mrs. Coleman, Prof. Kiddle, Dr. Everett and Mrs. Morrell. Franklin Clark, Secretary of the organization, wrote in the *Banner of Light,* 29 June 1889, "…that the great central principle of all life and being, whether it be called universal brotherhood, charity or love, should be made the rule of each one, that a condition of harmony and mutual helpfulness might be inaugurated and maintained on all the planes of human life and endeavor."

The *Banner of Light,* 27 September 1890, wrote, "It seems to be part of the spiritual work and the province of Mrs. Wallace to thus gather the friends of and workers in the Cause of Spiritualism beneath her hospitable roof, where all who enter feel the high and pure spiritual influence that pervades her home, and thus bring them into closer bonds of spiritual fellowship, and cultivate the social element which is so greatly needed in its ranks."

During the 1890s, Mrs. Wallace was a guest at Lily Dale, spoke at the funeral of Margaret Fox, and attended the Lake Brady Spiritualist camp. In 1892, she traveled to London. After returning home, she had regular meetings and seances at her home at 222 W. 59th Street, New York City.

Mrs. Wallace spoke to the School of Psychic Philosophy. The *Light of Truth,* 21 January 1899, wrote, "Mrs. M. E. Wallace, the well-known inspirational speaker, who held the audience enthralled while she discoursed on the beauty and helpfulness of the cause." In 1899, she attended the 51st anniversary meeting of the First Association of Spiritualists of New York. "After an opening song, Mrs. M. E. Wallace invoked the spirits at some length."

In 1917, Mrs. Wallace was a Women's War Relief organization volunteer in Brooklyn. The date of her passing is unknown.

GEORGE H. WALSER

George H. Walser was born in Dearborn County, Indiana in 1834, and was admitted to the Illinois bar in 1856. He married Harriet Cunningham in 1860 and then served in the 12th Illinois Infantry Regiment during the Civil War, commissioned a Lieutenant Colonel. He and Harriet had a son, Mark who was born in Illinois in 1863. After they moved to Barton County, Missouri, where George continued to practice law, they had a daughter, Lena in 1871.

In the late 1800's George published, *Orthopadeia or Atomic Solutions*, *Poems of Leisure, The Bouquet*, and other works. He and Harriet must have been divorced, for George married Alice Martha Newman in 1895. Martha died in 1902, and George married a third time to Esther Josephine Blount the same year.

The *St. Louis Post-Dispatch*, 26 August 1894, published an opinion piece by C. E. Chapin, entitled: "Spook Fakir's Camp Drew Crowds to Liberal, MO." Chapin referred to George as "high priest Walser." The cottages and tents well filled at the time and conferences and seances large. "Long-haired men and short-haired women have come from all over the western states, from Michigan, Minnesota and Texas, and some from as far away as the Pacific coast." Chapin explained that a dozen years before, George Walser had colonized the place with infidels and free lovers. He was a successful lawyer and once a member of the Missouri legislature. After becoming an atheist, he amassed a fortune by dealing in government lands and owned 4,000 acres in Barton County.

George went to Clinton on business and a friend invited him to a séance. He saw the spirit of his father and was convinced to become a Spiritualist. He converted twenty acres into a park. Catalpa trees, fountains, lakes and flowers. He built himself a home in the park as well as a dining hall and amphitheater that would seat 1,500 called the Celestial Dome.

Four years later, *The Sedalia Democrat,* 30 August 1898, complained about the camp. "Capt. Walser used to be a resident of this city (Lamar) but being averse to religion he went into the country and founded a town in which he declared religion would not be tolerated. For many years he and a small number of others lived almost in seclusion, as the town would not thrive. It was spoken as the Godless town of Liberal." The article continued, "Many good people shunned the place. Realizing the condition, the residents petitioned the M.E. conference to send them a minister, promising him a building for services and support, since which the town has prospered."

In 1910, George died in Liberal. The *Cedar County Republican* (Stockton, Missouri) wrote, "Religiously, Col. Walser was queer, be he possessed many of those qualities which make a man likable."

WILBUR S. WANDELL

Wilbur S. Wandell was born in 1847 in Michigan, the son of William and Eliza Wandell. His life had barely begun when his father died in 1852. Wilbur's first marriage was to Callie Norton before 1870 when she was a teenager. Wilbur worked as a carpenter in Kalamazoo, and they had two daughters, Grace and Maude. There is no record of a divorce, but Callie lived with her daughter Grace in Battle Creek, Michigan until her death in 1913, keeping the name Wandell and saying she was married.

Wilbur married Nancy Waugh in Morrow County, Ohio in 1895. They lived in Fairfield County, Ohio in 1900 with their son, Joy. Their daughter Elizabeth was born before they moved to Fresno, California before 1910.

Wilbur was active in facilitating Spiritualist camp meetings in Michigan and Ohio before he moved to Fresno. In 1887, he oversaw the camp meeting at Frazers' Grove in Vicksburg, Michigan. He reported that active efforts made the camp meeting at that place a great success for the season. In 1890 and 1891, he was president of the Vicksburg Spiritualists' Religious Association which had been running Frazer's Grove camp meeting since 1883.

He was also known as a meeting pioneer who ran the Spiritualist camp association in Ashley, Delaware county Ohio in 1890. The *Light of Truth*, 4 March 1893, published a piece by Samuel Waugh which described a séance in Ashley, Ohio that was attended by Waugh's family, Mr. W. S. Wandell, the medium's manager, and Benjamin F. Foster, the medium. In 1897, Wilbur was a delegate when they formed the Association of Ohio Spiritualists. By that time, he was living in the Spiritualist community, Summerland Beach, in California.

The family was living in Fresno, California in 1910. Wilbur was a plumber, and member of the Spiritualist church, IOOF lodge and Knights of Pythias Lodge. He died in 1928 following an illness of several weeks at age of 79. Nannie was still alive in 1950 and lived with her daughter, Elizabeth, in Fresno.

IDA P. A. WHITLOCK

Ida P. Andrews was born about 1852 to fish dealer, Francis, and Sarah Andrews. She married Fred O. Smith, a jeweler, in 1874 when he was 25 and she was 23. They had a daughter, Francis (Fannie) who was born in 1876, but the marriage did not last long. By 1880, Ida was living at home with her parents, daughter, and two brothers, in Providence, Rhode Island. The census recorded that she was divorced.

In 1884, Mrs. Ida P. Andrews Smith married Lewis L. Whitlock according to the *Boston Evening Transcript*. The couple, from Providence, Rhode Island, were given a party, according to the *Banner of Light*, the following year. L.L. Whitlock was editor of Facts Publishing Company and very active in with Spiritualism the Boston area. Ida was active in her own circles.

The *Banner of Light*, 5 September 1891, reported on Ida at the Onset Bay meeting. "After reading a poem conveying the thought that we are 'only remembered by what we have done,' she proceeded to speak upon 'Spiritualism and Its Relation to the World's Growth and Development.' Spiritualism, she said combines religion and philosophy. It has demonstrated the fact that there is no death, and that those who have passed from this into the other life can and do return. The phenomena of Spiritualism are the working-tools of our profession. They do not come into the world as playthings, but as educators—something more than to teach that man lives beyond the death of the physical body."

During the 1890s, Ida was a speaker at many meetings in New England and New York. She attended Lily Dale and National Spiritualist Conventions as well as the Providence Spiritualist Association events. The titles of her lectures included: "Faith without Works is Dead," "The

New Heaven and the New Life," and "The Spread of Spiritual Philosophy."

In the *Banner of Light,* 28 October 1893, Ida wrote that she was in Buffalo. "During the month of September, it was my privilege and pleasure to speak to the First Spiritualist Society of this city." She continued. "I was very much impressed with the interest manifested by young people, many of whom came to me after the meeting and said they were earnestly seeking light, by forming a circle for the development of the mediumistic gifts which different ones had learned they possessed."

Ida was also President of the Ladies' Industrial Society in Boston, advertised as a Psychometrist who gave readings from a lock of hair and handwriting, was a state agent for the Rhode Island National Spiritualist Association, and was known in Maine as a speaker and psychometric reader. She travelled to England at least twice in the early 1900s, and after being widowed moved in with her brothers in Providence. Her brother Frank was also active in the Spiritualist community. By 1930, she was living with her daughter Frances Dixon, both widowed, in Manhattan.

REV. FREDERICK A. WIGGIN

Rev. Frederick A. Wiggin was born in New Hampshire in 1858. Educated in the Baptist faith, he became actively engaged in the Baptist ministry. He married his wife Mabel in 1884. They lived in Luftonborough in 1900 and had two children, Edith and William. By 1903, they were living in Boston. He was pastor of the Unity Church, and Mrs. Wiggin was holding meetings of the Ladies' Auxiliary of the Boston Spiritual Temple at her home.

In 1907, he married his second wife, Jeanette. Frederick was a prominent pastor in Boston society. In 1914, he attracted about 1,100 people at the National Spiritualist Association meeting in Boston where he discussed orthodoxy. According to *The Boston Globe*, 10 Oct 1914, he said, "I prophesy that orthodox churches of all lands will in time be forced to employ the phenomena of spiritualism as it is employed on the platform, or the church structure will fall. Even now that is done by clergymen for the purpose of consoling the bereaved. Modern spiritualism in its best light is practically identical with Christianity." Wiggin was listed as a psychic, medium and public speaker at the events he attended.

Frederick served for 18 consecutive years at Camp Onset Bay and 16 years at Lily Dale. He also worked at many other camps: Etna, Temple Heights, Lakewood, Chesterfield, Lake Pleasant, and Freeville. Toward the end of his life, he attended Camp Silver Belle in Ephrata, Pennsylvania.

In 1920, he married his third wife, Ethel. He died twenty years later in July of 1940. The *Psychic Observer*, no. 53, 25 November 1940, wrote that during a séance at Camp Silver Belle in Ephrata, Pennsylvania, "Dr Frederick A Wiggin's voice was heard. He spoke at length and those recognizing his characteristic phraseology and speech say that it was just as if he had been standing before them—delivering one of his inimitable addresses."

MRS. MARY E. WILLIAMS

Although newspapers reported on Mrs. Mary E. Williams numerous times, her history is cloaked in mystery. There is a mention of a daughter, Cora in 1891, but it's unclear where Mary was born, when she died and who she may have been married to.

By the 1880s, Mary was an active medium in New York City, being notorious in both positive and negative ways. In *Medium and Daybreak,* 21 August 1885, Charles Day wrote that Mary was a leading medium having regular seances in New York in her parlors. Two of her spirits guides were, Crowfoot, an Indian Chief, and Papa Holland. He described the elegantly furnished parlor, with about 20 ladies and gentlemen attending, that contained a cabinet that was commonly used at the time. "The lady, becoming apparently semi-conscious, stepped into the cabinet, that was two curtains suspended on one side of the parlor. In a few minutes, after a little singing by the audience, a bell rang inside the curtains, and a lady of the house, who afterwards acted as reporter, taking down remarks of the materialized spirits, announced the arrival of a spirit."

In 1885, Mary began publishing *The New York Beacon Light.* Beacon lights were a form of early electric lighting for theater performances at the time. The *Religio-Philosophical Journal* noted that "The journal was the work of Mrs. M. E. ("Minnie") Williams, a long-lived and rather notorious New York materializing medium. She was the vehicle for a variety of spirits, including a Mr. Holland (a philosopher), Bright Eyes (a baby), Priscilla (a spinster), and Henry Ward Beecher, and was said to produce 30-40 materialized forms at a single seance." In 1889, she gave seances at Gilsey House and was paid large sums by George W. Kidd.

During the 1890s, Mary was a guest at the First Society of Spiritualists and lectured about Abraham Lincoln as a spiritualist at the First

Spiritualist church of New York. It was the largest gathering ever for the church. She gained more notoriety in 1891 when the second wife and widow of a wealthy entrepreneur, John Anderson, sold Mary her house valued at $25,000 for $1.00. That became part of several properties she owned in the city.

At that time, she was president of the Spiritualistic Society that met at Adelphi Hall. *The Evening World*, 10 February 1891, wrote, "Mrs. Williams is a most magnetic woman. She is perhaps thirty-five years old, tall, full-figured and handsome. Not pretty, nor beautiful—but handsome. She has an intellectual cast of features and is obliged to wear glasses. She is a painfully nervous woman, but withal a pleasant person, speaking directly to the point in a manly, businesslike way, though with that indescribable something that makes the woman charming." The article continued quoting her, "If Spiritualists were treated by the press with the same fairness and honesty that other earnest, honest investigators are, there would be more encouragement, both for the Spiritualists and the rest of the world."

There was always some question about the legitimacy of Mary's mediumship. *The Evening World*, 8 November 1894, ran a story from Paris, France, writing, "Mrs. Mary Williams from New York has arranged seances in St Petersburg, Berlin and The Hague after Paris. Mrs. Williams arrived by the steamship Bourgogne, Oct. 21, accompanied by her manager, Mr. Macdonald. She stopped at the boarding-house of Mme. Raulet, on Rue Hamelin." People were suspicious during her séance and laid a trap. One person seized a spirit and found it to be a doll. They also found Mrs. Williams to be in men's clothing. She fled to London, "Claiming that she had been trapped wickedly and made the victim of a horrible plot." had transferred the house in forty-sixth street to Mrs. Williams for the consideration of $1." *The Post Star*, 3 December 1894, wrote, "The exercises at Psychical hall yesterday afternoon consisted mainly of a defense of Mrs. M. E. Williams, the medium who was recently exposed in Paris." No details were given.

In 1899, a colony was being formed on Statin Island by the school of Psychic Philosophy organized in the spring of 1898. 150 acres on Meisner Avenue near the village of Richmond was bought. Wooden acres overlooking the lower bay were cleared to build cottages. Officers of the school include Mrs. M. E. Williams of Manhattan, President.

In 1904, Mary was in trouble with the law again. Detective Thomas Beet, paid for seances and charged her with obtaining money under false pretenses. She tried to get him to buy stocks during the seances, saying she was speaking for his father's spirit. If there was a conviction, it wasn't published.

From 1918 until 1922, Mary was inspirational lecturer, medium and then pastor at the First Spiritualist Church in New York City. There is no known record of her death.

Dr. Fred L. H. Willis

Fred Llewellyn Hovey Willis was born in 1830 in Cambridge, Massachusetts to Lorenzo and Eleanor Willis. She died in childbirth. He knew many writers including Emerson, Fuller and Alcott. They founded Brook Farm in West Roxbury, Massachusetts as an idealistic social democracy location where Hawthorne did his first literary work.

The Brooklyn Daily Eagle, 13 April 1885 told Fred's story of becoming involved with Spiritualism, "I was a young man of twenty-one years when I first felt the manifestations which have since become so familiar. I had left Cambridge temporarily for the benefit of my health, and was voyaging to South America. Sea sickness seized me violently and I kept to my stateroom during the earlier part of the voyage. By and by I began to notice strange things transpiring in my little stateroom—for instance knockings—and frequently invisible hands touching me. When I became well again, I thought that these things were merely the delusions of sickness, but when I arrived at Rio Janeiro, I soon found that some subtle changes had taken place in me which had developed some previously unknown powers of my soul, if you please. I could tell what people were thinking of by looking at them, and I knew if a person was writing to me and what he or she was writing about. Other spiritualistic phenomena happened about me, but I fought off the notion of its being of supernatural origin till I returned to Boston." Later he said, "I had never previously had any medical knowledge at all except a smattering which one picks up in the public schools. In the hands of the spirits, however, I became an old man with a perfect knowledge of medicine."

Fred's interest in Spiritualism caused problems at first. According to the *Spiritual Telegraph*, 2 May 1857, "The case of Mr. Willis, a suspended Divinity student at Cambridge, is creating an unusual ferment among the clergy of Boston and vicinity; and the excitement is rapidly spreading in all directions, and among all classes of people. Mr. Willis is a remarkable medium for physical manifestation; and at a recent sitting at which Professor Eustis of Cambridge Faculty was present, Mr. Willis' foot and the Professor's came in contact under the table; when the learned Professor seized Mr. Willis' limb, and accused it, or its owner, of deception. This led to the suspension, on the part of the faculty of the College, of Mr. Willis."

Reverend Thomas Higginson who attended the meeting said that the accusations were not proven. He published his observations about musical instruments located under the table being played and moved, and an accordion on Fred's lap playing tunes at request of the attendees. Higginson witnessed faint lights that appeared on the table and other lights flickering around the room. The accordion played when it was on Mr. Higginson's lap, out of Fred's reach. He also saw a guitar play without anyone touching it and felt hands grasping his feet, but he wasn't sitting close to Fred.

After graduating from Harvard Divinity School, Fred was ordained a Unitarian minister. He lived in Michigan where he abandoned the ministry to enter the Homeopathic Medical School in New York City. He married Love Whitcomb of New Hampshire in 1858, and they had a daughter while he practiced medicine in Elmira and Glendora, New York.

Fredrick was an active medical medium while in Michigan in the late 1850s and 1860s. In the *Spiritual Times*, 2 July 1864, in a quote from the *Banner of Light*, Fred wrote, "We do not need to go back and say how old dogmas dissolve, and how, one by one, the superstitions of the past leave us free and untrammeled to search for great principles, and to aspire after divine truths. They leave us—these errors—naturally, and the benign inspirations of heaven take their place. We no longer stand divorced from the Eternity of God—we dwell in it. And now our hearts open themselves and express their sympathetic oneness with the true, the pure, and the good."

Fred and Love lived in New York Coty for a time. While there, they were editors for the weekly publication, *The Present Age*, from 1868 until1873. The publication was "devoted to the Spiritual Philosophy, Polite Literature and General Intelligence, and the Reformatory Movements of the Day." Suffrage for was Women Specially Advocated.

During the 1870s and 1880s, Fred's lecture topics included: "Woman's Place in the World of Ideas," "The Light of the Soul and Jesus of Nazareth," "The Heaven and Hell of Spiritualism versus those of Theology," "The Philosophy of Evil," "The Inner Life," and "The Growth of the Spirit." In 1871, the Music Hall Free Spiritual Meeting in Boston featured his talk about his spiritual experience in Naples and Rome.

Fred's continued to lecture in the 1890s in New England and New York state., including Lily Dale and Rochester, New York. He was known as an inspirational healer and speaker. In 1900, he stayed in Rochester, New York, giving a course of parlor lectures on "Metaphysics or the Science of the Human Soul."

At the time of his death in 1914, Fred was living with his daughter and was a member of the Unitarian Church. He had had a summer home in Glendora on Seneca Lake for forty years.

MRS. M. S. TOWNSEND WOOD

Melvina S. Holt was born in Woodstock, Vermont in 1828 to Dr. Jacob M. and Susan E. Holt who settled in Bridgewater, Vermont. Melvina had one sister, Flora E. Holt Newton. The family apparently took an early interest in Spiritualism. A Spiritualists Memorial to Congress sent in March 1854 to the 33rd Congress stated, "Memorial of N. P. Tallmadge and others, Citizens of the US praying the appointment of a Scientific Commission to investigate certain physical and mental phenomena of questionable origin and mysterious import that have of late occurred in this country and in Europe." It was signed by Jacob M. Holt and Susan E. Holt of Bridgewater among hundreds of others.

By 1856, Melvina was listed as a medium in Bridgewater, Vermont as Mrs. M. S. Townsend (formerly Mrs. Newton). She was advertised as giving clairvoyant examinations and sittings for friends in the towns she was visiting. She was also called a trance medium in 1859. Her father was listed as a healer in 1860 and 1861.

Melvina's marriages are not well documented. In 1866, she was called Mrs. M. S. Townsend of Bridgewater, Vermont; in 1868 and 1872 Mrs. M. S. Townsend Hoadley of Vermont; and in 1876 Mrs. M. S. Townsend of Cambridge Port, Massachusetts. The only marriage record found is to farmer Charles N. Wood in 1877. It was his second marriage and her third according to the document. They lived in Newton, Massachusetts.

Throughout the late 1870s and 1880s, Melvina spoke to large audiences. From 1879-1887, she was on the *Banner of Light's* list for Spiritualist speakers. At the Lake Pleasant Spiritualist camp, she spoke on "The General Features of Spiritualism." She also participated at the Labor Reform Convention in Boston in 1880.

The *Fitchburg Sentinel*, 14 April 1882 wrote, "Mrs. Townsend Wood, one of the oldest and best speakers in the field, is to speak for the Leominster Spiritualists...." During the 1880s, she was guest speaker at Camp Etna, Onset Bay Camp, and spoke in other New England towns. The titles of her talks included "The Prison, the Gallows and the Philosophy of Charity," and "The Power of Spirit over Matter."

She was also a proponent of suffrage and prohibition. In 1888, at Onset Bay, "That grand advocate of woman suffrage and prohibition, Mrs. Townsend-Wood, was speaker of the forenoon. Her subject, 'Temperance, and its relation to Spiritualism,' was ably handled," wrote the *Golden Gate*, 28 July 1888.

Her husband, Charles Wood, died in 1905 and Melvina followed in 1907. In her will she said she would like either to be cremated in Massachusetts or buried in Vermont without clothes so that the clothing did not go to waste. She was cremated in Cambridge, Massachusetts.

FRANCIS B. WOODBURY

Francis B. Woodbury was born in Bolton, Massachusetts in 1857, the son of Frank M. and Julia Bailey Woodbury. His father was no longer living in 1870, and he is living in Bolton, Massachusetts with his mother and brother at mother's parents' farm. By 1880, he had moved to Middlesex, Massachusetts and was living with cousins while working as a telephone clerk. He married eight years later at Bulfinch Place Unitarian Church to Annie L Clark, and they made their home at 23 Bromley Street in Roxbury.

While residing in Roxbury, Francis was elected secretary at the annual National Spiritualists Association meetings, 1894-1897. He wrote to the *Buffalo News*, 18 April 1895, about their statement that Spiritualism was not expanding. "The fact is that spiritualism is progressing rapidly all over the world, and there has been a very large number of societies organized in the last three months and one of our weekly papers gained 2000 subscribers in that time."

The *Progressive Thinker*, 3 October 1896, wrote, "The efficient secretary, Francis B. Woodbury, has been a prominent worker in Spiritualistic circles for nearly twenty years, and the charge of inexperience and over-zealous youth cannot be laid at his door." His wife, Annie, was also involved with Spiritualism. At an 1896 meeting in Boston, she gave tests and readings. She also attended Massachusetts Convention of Spiritualists in February.

Francis was elected secretary at the Annual Convention of National Spiritualists Association in 1897, an important year for women's rights. "Two-thirds of the audience at to-day's sessions of the National Spiritualist Association (NSA) were women." That year, resolutions were adopted looking to the "liberation of women," setting out that women had been "kept long enough in the position of Indians or idiots, and that women had helped for centuries to build up homes without having partnership."

The *Lawrence Daily Journal*, 30 December 1897, wrote that the Francis spoke at the NSA meeting in Cleveland. They wrote, "He said that so-called magicians did things which mediums accomplished, but the former resorted to trickery, while the power of the later was due to spiritual influence. He said there is little difference between the mesmeric and trance conditions, and, inasmuch as there was no doubt about the genuineness of the former, there should be no doubt about the latter."

Francis was voted out as NSA Secretary in 1898 but continued to participate. He gave addresses at the Lookout Mountain Spiritualist camp, discussed the history of the organization, and was concerned with people being arrested for their beliefs.

Frances and Annie lived in Greenfield, Massachusetts in 1900 where he worked as a night watchman, and she was a waitress. They had a daughter, Ruth, and later moved to the nearby Spiritualist community of Lake Pleasant. Francis became involved in politics, supporting the Democratic Party and became secretary for Lake Pleasant Independent Order of Scalpers.

In 1915, Francis joined the Unitarian church in Springfield, Massachusetts. He was a delegate at the Unitarian meeting in 1920 and The Church of Unity Treasurer in 1921. By 1923, he was the Springfield First Spiritualist Church President and in 1924 sexton at the Church of Unity.

Francis died in Springfield, Massachusetts in 1924. At the time, he had been a resident there for 18 years He was a member of the Church of Unity and the United Order of Workmen. Annie and Ruth Dionne were still living.

JULIETTE YEAW

Juliette Hills was born in 1831 in Leominster, Massachusetts to Emerson and Susannah Hills. She married Asher A. D. Yeaw in 1853 and they had three children: William, Arthur and Catherine. Juliette's speaking engagements began when her children were very young. Beginning in 1867, she was listed in the *Banner of Light* as a Spiritualist lecturer living in Northborough, Massachusetts. She spoke throughout the state and in Rhode Island for the next decade. Asher became employed in a comb shop around 1880, and they moved to Worchester, Massachusetts.

By 1879, Juliette was listed as a speaker at the Lake Pleasant camp meeting. She would continue lecturing for many camp meetings including Ocean Grove, Harwich Port, Sunapee Lake and Queen City Park during the 1880s. At the Mediums' Camp-meeting of the Two Worlds, *Spirit Voices*, July 1885, wrote, "Mrs. Juliette Yeaw in the afternoon held a large audience spell-bound with the eloquence of the old veteran spirit-friend A.T. Foss, that controlled her. Her subject was, 'Is Spiritualism True?' and a finer discourse never came from mortal lips." The *Golden Gate*, 17 November 1888, wrote about her lectures at Queen City Park. "Mrs. Yeaw is a lady possessed of superior natural talent, highly intuitive and inspirational, and carries with her that charm of perfect loveliness only presented by those who lead the higher life."

In 1894, Juliette was ordained and installed as pastor of the Independent Liberal Church at Greenwich. In 1899, she was a speaker at the Massachusetts State Association of Spiritualists' 51st anniversary celebration. She was also a member of the Women's Suffrage league, elected president in 1902.

The *Banner of Light*, 6 January 1906, asked people to write their plans for the New Year. Juliette wrote: "The gulf between the things which I would like to do in the New Year and the things I can do, does not prevent my bridging the chasm with good intentions, which admit of my saying, I would like to open the doors of Waverly House and see it fully equipped for the noble service for which it was designed." She wanted to make sure that those who wanted to read spiritualistic papers could get them. She also wanted to help the Morris Pratt Institute, encourage struggling mediums, offer greater comfort to the bereaved, and make the New Year the best of her life.

In 1910, Asher was 81 and Juliette was 78. They were living at home with their daughter and one son. Juliette died in 1915 from heart disease at the age of 84. Asher survived her.

AUTHORS

Reverend Karen Heasley

Karen Heasley had a near death experience at the age of five when she died on the operating table. Because of that experience, she has been conscious of the spirit world since that time. After her parents passed, she was drawn to mediumship. She studied under two great mediums: Reverend Leonard Young, a British medium who taught at Arthur Findlay College at Stansted and Reverend Janet Nohavec who leads The Journey Within Church in New Jersey, USA.

Karen is trained in evidential and platform mediumship and opened her own church, The Spiritual Path Church in New Castle, Pennsylvania, USA. The church is affiliated with the Spiritualist National Union. She is also a member of the Lily Dale Assembly and the International Association for Near-Death Studies.

Susan Urbanek Linville

Susan Linville received a PhD in biology from the University of Dayton and has lectured as adjunct faculty. She has administrative experience as an assistant editor for a science journal, university outreach coordinator, and history museum assistant administrator. As a freelance writer, she has published short fiction, newspaper and magazine articles, non-fiction books, and was a script writer for Indiana University's *A Moment of Science* Podcast Series. Along with scientific research and lab manuals, her books include memoirs and locally published history. Her most notable is: *A School for My Village*, Twesigye Jackson Kaguri & Susan Urbanek Linville, 2011, Penguin Books.

Other Books:

Treasures from the Spirit World

Spiritualist Camps

Seers, Mediums and Spiritualists

www.ingramcontent.com/pod-product-compliance
Lightning Source LLC
Chambersburg PA
CBHW051816090426
42736CB00011B/1513